THE STATUE OF LIBERTY

The STATUE of LIBERTY

★ *Birth to Rebirth*

BY SUE BURCHARD

ILLUSTRATED WITH PHOTOGRAPHS

HBJ HARCOURT BRACE JOVANOVICH, PUBLISHERS

San Diego   New York   London

The author and publisher wish to express their appreciation to George Rush for permission to reprint on pages 131–135 material from his article on Superintendent Dave Moffitt from *Esquire*, July 1982; and to *The New York Times* to reprint on page 126 material from Murray Schumach's article, "Ranger Ends Idyll with Famed Lady," Copyright © 1969 by The New York Times Company. Reprinted by permission.

Photo credits appear on page 200.

Printed in the United States of America

Design by Barbara DuPree Knowles

LIBRARY OF CONGRESS CATALOGING IN PUBLICATION DATA
Burchard, Sue.
The Statue of Liberty.
Bibliography: p.
 SUMMARY: Traces the history of the Statue of Liberty from its conception to its centennial with emphasis on the statue's restoration, its significance through the years, and the plans for the 1986 centennial celebration.
 1. Statue of Liberty (New York, N.Y.)—Juvenile literature. 2. Statue of Liberty National Monument (New York, N.Y.)—Juvenile literature. 3. New York (N.Y.)—Buildings, structures, etc.—Juvenile literature. [1. Statue of Liberty (New York, N.Y.) 2. National monuments. 3. Statues.] I. Title.
F128.64.L6B87 1985   974.7'1   85-5525

ISBN 0-15-279969-9   C D E

CONTENTS

INTRODUCTION   vii

1 / A VISIT TO THE STATUE *(1985)*   3

2 / THE BIRTH OF AN IDEA *(1865–1871)*   13

3 / LIBERTY BECOMES A REALITY *(1871–1878)*   23

4 / THREE GENIUSES AT WORK *(1878–1884)*   36

5 / LIBERTY ARRIVES IN AMERICA *(1884–1886)*   45

6 / HER FIRST YEARS *(1886–1890)*   58

7 / LIBERTY AS THE "MOTHER OF EXILES" *(1890–1900)*   64

8 / A NEW ROLE FOR LIBERTY *(1900–1920)*   77

9 / LIBERTY BECOMES
    A NATIONAL MONUMENT *(1920–1932)*   85

10 / THE STATUE TURNS FIFTY *(1932–1940)*   91

11 / THE WAR AND ITS AFTERMATH *(1940–1950)*   103

12 / THE MASTER PLAN IS COMPLETED *(1950–1960)*   113

13 / THE TROUBLED SIXTIES *(1960–1970)*   118

14 / PROTESTS AND A CELEBRATION *(1970–1980)*   127

15 / A CLIMB LEADS
TO RESTORATION PLANS *(1980–1982)*   136

16 / THE PEOPLE COME
TO THE RESCUE AGAIN *(1982–1984)*   153

17 / THE LADY TURNS ONE HUNDRED *(1984–1986)*   169

LIBERTY'S MEASUREMENTS   184

CHRONOLOGY OF IMPORTANT EVENTS   186

ACKNOWLEDGMENTS   189

BIBLIOGRAPHY   191

INDEX   195

PHOTO CREDITS   200

INTRODUCTION

Americans began counting the birthdays of the Statue of Liberty after she had been assembled in this country on a tiny island in New York harbor, but the story of the statue actually began long before the rainy dedication ceremony on Bedloe's Island on October 28, 1886. The idea was conceived at a French dinner party in 1865, and it took twenty-one years for the idea to become a reality. This book traces the history of the Statue of Liberty over a period of 121 years—from the birth of the idea to Liberty's one hundredth birthday. As you read the story, I think you will agree that the one-hundred-year-old lady has led a fascinating and often exciting life.

THE STATUE OF LIBERTY

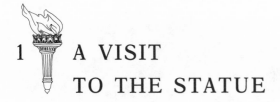

1 A VISIT
TO THE STATUE

On a cold but bright and sunny day in January 1985, a group of about forty people gathered at the southern tip of New York City in an area known as Battery Park. Most of them were not New Yorkers. Some were tourists from Michigan and Alabama. Almost half were visitors from foreign countries.

Although they dressed differently and spoke different languages, the one thing these men, women, and children had in common was their desire to see the Statue of Liberty. They were all buying a two-dollar round-trip ticket for the 1:00 P.M. ferry. From their places in the ticket line, they could see the statue half facing them on a small oval-shaped island one and two-thirds miles out in New York harbor.

It took only a few minutes for the group to board the large ferry that could hold 460 people. As the boat pulled away from the dock, several Japanese tourists lined the railing and had their pictures taken with the Manhattan skyline, including the World Trade Center, as a background.

During the ten-minute boat ride, total strangers chatted freely. The knowledge that they were all sharing the adventure of taking a boat ride in the dead of winter to visit a world-wide symbol

The Statue of Liberty ferry docked at Battery Park

Two children from different countries get acquainted on the way to the Statue of Liberty.

of democracy and freedom somehow made them relaxed and comfortable with each other.

A five-year-old child speaking French stood at the rail and offered potato chips to a little blonde girl standing next to her. At first the blonde child was frightened by the strange language, but soon the two children had figured out a way to communicate and were laughing and playing together.

Just before the ferry approached Liberty Island, a voice over the loudspeaker announced that the boat was passing Ellis Island, which had become an official part of the Statue of Liberty National Monument in 1965. The two islands, Liberty and Ellis, so closely linked in history, are now both under the care of the National Park Service.

Almost everyone aboard the ferry moved to the starboard rail to catch a glimpse of the ruins of the most famous immigration center in the United States, where starting in 1892 twelve to sixteen million people were either allowed to enter this strange new land or were rejected and sent back. Probably many people on the ferry had ancestors who had landed there. The guide went on to explain that the Ellis Island immigration center had closed down in 1954, when the tide of immigrants had almost come to a halt, and had been abandoned for thirty years. It was obvious that the buildings were in a sad state of disrepair, that weeds covered the lawns, and that some of the docks had collapsed.

Almost immediately after passing Ellis Island, the ferry drew close to Liberty Island. The passengers turned their eyes from the buildings of Ellis Island to the enormous green statue totally surrounded by metal scaffolding, the torch missing from her upraised right hand. The visitors were treated to several different views as the ferry rounded the island close to the shoreline. Again everyone rushed for a spot along the railing, this time to be photographed with the famous lady in the background.

Pictures taken, the group stared at the orange elevator moving slowly up to the top of the right upraised hand and watched openmouthed as workmen stepped carefully out onto metal beams 305 feet high in the air.

As they disembarked, the visitors were given instructions over a loudspeaker system in English, Spanish, Japanese, and French. A few National Park Service employees and the island's friendly bomb-sniffing dog, Tally, greeted the visitors.

As the guests moved out onto a wide tree-lined walk cutting across the width of the island, they observed on their left the National Park Service administration building. Beyond it was a fenced-in area where the tourists could see a lawn and many trees that supplied shade in warmer months and protection from harbor winds in the winter. Institutional-looking brick buildings provide living quarters for the island staff, and a sign on the fence reads, "Area closed to the public."

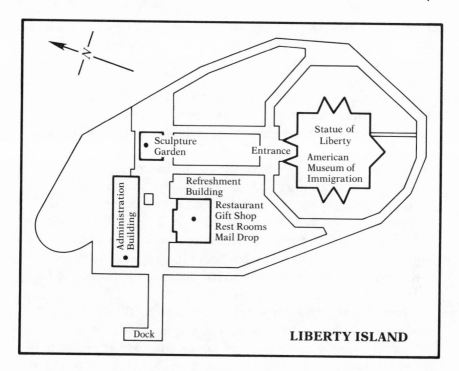

LIBERTY ISLAND

The rest of Liberty Island, however, was open to visitors. Some people stopped at a building on the right housing a gift shop, restaurant, and rest rooms. No one that day was brave enough to eat in the outdoor refreshment area.

Visitors who continued along found themselves in a small sculpture garden containing statues of Joseph Pulitzer, Alexander Gustave Eiffel, Frédéric Auguste Bartholdi, Édouard de Laboulaye, and Emma Lazarus—people who had played an important part in the Statue of Liberty's history.

Beyond the sculpture garden is a broad promenade along the water's edge lined with several mounted binoculars, where the visitors were able to deposit coins and get a close-up view of

Workmen ride an elevator to the top of the caged lady.

Ellis Island and the southern tip of Manhattan Island. Running from the sculpture garden to the statue are two avenues. These walks enclose a large fenced-in lawn used for ceremonies and celebrations.

The statue has her back turned to visitors approaching her from the island walks. She faces those who arrive by sea. Upon entering the monument on this particular day, visitors were greeted by yet another loudspeaker voice announcing that a puppet show was about to begin on the balcony level.

Families with young children and a school group climbed the steps to the balcony and settled themselves before a portable puppet stage. A handsome park ranger wearing his Smokey Bear hat stepped before the audience. When the curtains parted, he introduced himself and two Muppet-type puppets named Polly and Bernard. Bernard was worried because the Statue of Liberty "looks as if she is in a cage."

The ranger, with Polly's help, explained to Bernard and the audience that the statue is ninety-eight years old and has taken a beating from wind, rain, and time. The cage is scaffolding erected so that repairs can be made to make her as good as new for her one hundredth birthday on October 28, 1986. He told the children that the best present they could give the statue was to help take care of her. The program ended with everybody singing, "Happy Birthday, Dear Miss Liberty."

The visitors, particularly the children, were disappointed that they could not climb the 171 spiral steps leading from the base of the statue to the crown viewing area, but there were plenty of other things to see and do on Liberty Island that day. Movies telling about the history of the Statue of Liberty and Ellis Island were shown every hour.

By the time the visitors progressed to the American Museum of Immigration, circular in layout and located in the foundation of the statue, another group of visitors had arrived by ferry. During the peak summer months about 2,000 visitors a day come to Liberty Island. The numbers are of course considerably less during the winter, but the statue stays open all year long.

In the museum the visitors entered darkened rooms where the history of immigration unfolded in a dramatic, chronological fashion through a series of huge photographs, dioramas, and life-sized wax figures dressed in period costumes. Children rushed to be the first to activate recordings telling segments of the moving history of Ellis Island.

"I feel as if I am in a cave," whispered one small visitor to his mother. Part of the space for the museum, his mother told him, had been laboriously drilled into the giant solid concrete foundation of the monument. Engineers did not dare risk using dynamite because the blasts might have caused harm to the pedestal and statue towering overhead. It is no wonder therefore that the museum has an underground, cave-like feeling to it.

After a tour of the museum, the ranger took the visitors outside to walk around the statue. He explained that the broken shackle chain lying near one end of Liberty's forward-striding left foot is supposed to convey the idea that she has stepped forward to break the chain of tyranny and slavery. A more practical reason for the forward striding left foot, however, is to provide balance for the upraised right hand. The book held in the statue's left hand, the ranger explained, represents the Declaration of Independence. The date of the nation's birth, July 4, 1776, is inscribed on it in Roman numerals.

The size of the lady towering over them impressed all the visitors. They gasped as the ranger informed them that her nose is four feet long, her mouth is three feet wide, one of her hands is eight feet long, and a single fingernail measures thirteen by ten inches.

The ranger then led the group around the statue and into a long building recently erected to serve as a workshop. There, in an enormous, high-ceilinged room filled with equipment, the work of building Liberty's new torch was taking place. Over a hundred years earlier the young French sculptor who designed the statue, Frédéric Auguste Bartholdi, had welcomed visitors to his workshop in Paris to observe the construction of the original statue. Now once again the public had been invited to watch, through a glass wall that ran the full length of the work-shop, the work on the reconstruction of the monument that was a gift from the people of France to the people of the United States to commemorate the alliance of the two countries during the American Revolution.

Many parts of the statue were being repaired with advanced modern technology. The new torch, however, was being con-structed by the same method used by Bartholdi himself—that is, by making a series of increasingly large plaster models. The visitors could see them in various sizes and could observe work-ers carefully applying a layer of plaster to the final model. A wooden frame would eventually be carefully molded around the final model and, when removed, would form a mold into which metal workers would hammer thin sheets of copper. These copper sheets would then be bolted together to form the new torch.

The old torch, the ranger explained, was on a countrywide tour, and the workmen were anxious to have it back in order to make additional measurements to ensure that the new torch would have the exact dimensions of the old one. As Bartholdi had wished, the new torch would not have any holes cut in it and would be gilded with gold. Light would shine on it rather than from it.

As soon as the torch was finished, the biggest job of the res-toration would begin, the visitors were told. The 1,500 ribs, each one different from the next, that make up the statue's skeleton had become badly rusted. One by one they would be taken down, copied in stainless steel, and carefully fitted back into place. It would be a long, demanding job, and more than a few of the visitors wondered if all the work could really be done by Lib-erty's one hundredth birthday.

As the afternoon drew to a close, the members of the group

The interior of the workshop at the base of Liberty, where a new torch is being constructed from a series of increasingly larger plaster models

who had arrived on the 1:00 P.M. ferry left to return to Manhattan, undoubtedly impressed by what they had seen. To the
foreigners, the statue was a symbol of America. To United States
citizens, she had been a reassuring symbol of liberty during two
great wars and was now regarded as a personal friend. It was
a little frightening to see at first hand how she might actually
collapse if something wasn't done.

What many of the passengers on the ferry did not know was
that throughout their histories the Statue of Liberty and Ellis
Island had encountered many problems. How they were solved
or not solved make quite a story. We shall start with the birth
of the idea and trace the Statue of Liberty's history to her rebirth
as a totally restored and refurbished monument.

Leaving the Statue of Liberty in the late afternoon

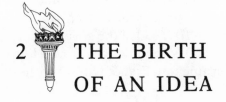

2 THE BIRTH
OF AN IDEA

The story begins at a dinner party where a man named Édouard de Laboulaye was talking about his favorite subject— the United States of America. He was speaking excitedly to a distinguished group of French intellectuals whom he had invited for dinner at his estate near Versailles, France. The year was 1865.

Laboulaye probably knew more about the United States than any other man in France at that time. He had written a large three-volume set of books about it. Ever since it had been discovered, America had seemed like a land of freedom and opportunity to many living in the Old World. Although the United States had just been through a civil war, the young democratic government had survived and, according to those present at the dinner party, was giving its people order and liberty. To Édouard de Laboulaye, these two things were the most important things in the world, and his goal in life was to see a similar kind of government set up in his own country.

Shortly after the United States won its freedom from England a revolution took place in France too, but it was a much bloodier one than the American revolution. The citizens of France formed a militia, the National Assembly drafted a constitution, and eventually the monarchy was abolished. King Louis XVI, his queen Marie Antoinette, and thousands of their followers were put to death, as well as many of the revolutionaries themselves as various factions strove for power.

In the years that followed, the French government and its leaders changed many times. At the time of the dinner party in 1865, an ambitious man, Napoleon III, headed the government. Laboulaye and his friends often talked of how they would like to see a republican form of government in France with a written constitution.

The men around the dinner table felt their destiny was somehow tied to that of the United States. France and the great French hero Lafayette had helped the United States win its freedom. Even more important to Laboulaye, however, was the fact that he felt the people of France and the United States were united in their love of liberty. He therefore suggested giving a gift of a giant statue to the United States—a gift that he hoped would strengthen the bond between the two countries and unite them in their commitment to democratic ideals.

"If a monument were to be built in America as a memorial to their independence, I should think it very natural if it were built by united efforts, if it were a common work of both nations," Laboulaye suggested to his friends.

These words made a great impression on one of the dinner guests, a thirty-one-year-old sculptor named Frédéric Auguste Bartholdi. Making monuments to war heroes and popular ideals was the thing to do in France at that time, and Bartholdi had been making patriotic statues for several years. He had received his first big commission when he was only eighteen years old and had built a large statue of Jean Rapp, a marshall in Napoleon's army, who had come from Colmar, a region of France near the German border, where Bartholdi had also lived as a child.

Basically, Auguste Bartholdi built very traditional statues, but several years earlier he had taken a trip to Egypt. He loved the country, and seeing the sphinx and the pyramids had left him with an obsession—to build a monument that was huge and would last forever. He therefore began thinking in terms of a rather colossal statue for his American monument. The time was not right, however, for such a project. Napoleon III was

Édouard de Laboulaye

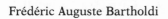

Frédéric Auguste Bartholdi

certainly not interested in making a gift to a country with a democratic form of government, particularly a gift with liberty as its theme. Bartholdi would have to wait.

In the meantime, he looked around for some other place to build such a statue. In his beloved Egypt the Suez Canal was just being completed. Bartholdi proposed building at the entrance to the canal a gigantic statue that would also serve as a lighthouse. The statue would be of a fellah many times life size, holding a torch. Fellahs were the peasants who provided the labor to build the canal. The theme for the monument would be "Progress" or "Egypt Carrying the Light to Asia." The Egyptian government seemed intrigued for a time but eventually lost interest and dropped the project.

Then events in France made Bartholdi give up his sculpting career for a while. In 1870 the Franco-Prussian War began. Bartholdi had no great love for Napoleon III, but he did love his country. He obtained a commission in the National Guard and a short time later secured a transfer from Paris to his native Colmar. The French, confident of victory, were totally surprised by the strength of the Germans, who quickly defeated their neighbor. Colmar fell into German hands.

Napoleon III was captured by the Germans, and the Third Republic was established in France. Shortly after Bartholdi resigned from the National Guard, Édouard de Laboulaye suggested that he make a trip to the United States. It might be a good time, Laboulaye felt, to further the cause of liberty by looking around for a place to build the American statue and by getting influential citizens to help pay for it. "Go to see that country," Laboulaye said. "You will study it. You will bring back your impressions."

Auguste Bartholdi had never been to America. In 1871, armed with a handful of letters to influential and important Americans, he set off on a ship to the United States. He was full of enthusiasm and hope. In those days a sculptor had to be good at raising money. Bartholdi was a terrific salesman, and he was firmly convinced that Americans would love his grand plan.

One of several sketches done by Auguste Bartholdi of a draped woman holding a torch on Bedloe's Island

As soon as Bartholdi saw tiny Bedloe's Island at the entrance to New York harbor, he knew he had found the perfect spot for his statue, and he immediately took out his sketchbook and began making drawings of a draped woman holding a torch in the air. One of his sketches had the uncompleted Brooklyn Bridge in the background. Critics later complained that Bartholdi's plan for the Statue of Liberty was a copy of the monument he had designed for the Suez Canal. Bartholdi said the two statues had nothing to do with each other, but there was no denying it. The two plans were very similar.

Some information about Bartholdi's first trip to America can be learned from letters he wrote to his mother. His father had died in 1836, when Bartholdi was two years old, and as a consequence he had always been very close and devoted to his mother. When he arrived on June 21 he wrote, "Everybody is running to and fro pressed by the stomach ache of business. It seems to me Americans don't know how to live. In New York there are 250 churches and 1,208 banks, one indistinguishable from another." Bartholdi felt Americans were more interested in getting rich than in having a good time or going to church.

Bartholdi could also see from looking around him that some people in the United States did not have liberty or the freedom to live as they pleased. Black slaves had been freed, but their terrible poverty kept them from being really free. Women did not have the right to vote. That very year 200,000 immigrants had come to the United States. They did not find the streets paved with gold as some had expected. Many ended up in city slums and had to take jobs working long hours for little pay.

Bartholdi observed these conditions as he traveled around the country, but he also saw that the United States of America was growing at an incredibly fast pace. In another letter to his mother he wrote, "Everything is big here. I am sure my statue will be at home in America."

New York City was a very busy place when Bartholdi visited it. This picture is of Hester Street in the late 1800s.

Laboulaye's letters of introduction opened doors for him, and he met many important people. In New York he met Horace Greeley, the editor of the *New York Tribune;* George William Curtis, the editor of *Harper's Weekly;* and Peter Cooper, a manufacturer and philantropist who helped pay for the trans-Atlantic cable. In Philadelphia he met Colonel John W. Forney, the influential publisher of the *Press.* He made several trips to Nahant, Massachusetts, to visit the great American poet Henry Wadsworth Longfellow.

To them all, Bartholdi spoke with fervor about his hopes for the new French republic and the statue he called "My American." He went to visit President Ulysses S. Grant at the summer White House in Long Branch, New Jersey, overlooking the Atlantic Ocean, and was startled when a passing ship saluted the President with a cannon blast. President Grant was fascinated by the enthusiasm of Bartholdi but offered no real support for the project.

Senator Charles Sumner of Massachusetts, chairman of the Senate Foreign Relations Committee, showed considerably more interest. He took the young sculptor to Washington and introduced him to many of his friends in Congress.

Bartholdi also spent some time visiting the home of the well-known American artist John LaFarge in Newport, Rhode Island. It was there he met a famous American architect, Richard Morris Hunt, the designer of the main building of the Metropolitan Museum of Art in New York City and of many mansions for members of society. Hunt would later play a part in Liberty's history. Bartholdi also met a young lady who was, like him, a visitor from France. Her name was Jeanne-Emilie Baheux de Puysieux. The two became close friends.

In August, Bartholdi began a trip across the United States. He made friends everywhere because he was full of enthusiasm for everyone and everything he saw. He went to Chicago and Omaha. He was overwhelmed by the vastness of the prairies, and he could hardly control his excitement when a huge buffalo herd held up his train for hours. The size of the Rocky Mountains

Richard Morris Hunt

amazed him. Even the American families were large, he discovered. After talking to Morman leader Brigham Young in Utah, he wrote a letter to his mother asking her to try to imagine a man who had sixteen wives and forty-nine children. In California he was almost as overcome with the wonder of the redwoods as he had been with the pyramids of Egypt.

By the time he left, having spent five months in America, Frédéric Auguste Bartholdi had made many friends and had very effectively spread word of his plans. No one, however, had offered to help pay for the project, but Bartholdi did not let this bother him. He left convinced the statue should be built on Bedloe's Island and should take the form of a Roman goddess holding a torch in the air. He even had a name for his statue, "Liberty Enlightening the World."

3 LIBERTY BECOMES A REALITY

When Bartholdi returned to France, the country was still in a state of political turmoil. Édouard de Laboulaye and his friends were eager to hear about the trip, but Laboulaye, who was a very keen politician, knew that a new form of government takes a number of years to become accepted and to begin to work effectively. He did not want to introduce the idea of the Statue of Liberty to the French people until he was quite sure they would accept it.

Therefore, Bartholdi had to wait several years to launch his Liberty project. During that time he worked out detailed plans for his colossal statue and was given a commission to create a monument of the Marquis de Lafayette to be given to the people of the United States in appreciation of American help during the Franco-Prussian War.

Finally, in 1874 the French Assembly completed a written constitution for the Third Republic. At last Laboulaye felt the government was sufficiently stable to permit talking in public about the idea of France's giving a great monument of liberty to the United States. Actual work, of course, could not begin on the statue until there was money to pay for it.

By late in the year it became clear that the French probably could not raise enough money for the entire monument and that the Americans would have to help finance their gift from France. A decision was made that the French would pay for the statue while the Americans would pay for the foundation and pedestal.

Under the leadership of Laboulaye, the French-American Union

Bartholdi's clay model for the statue

was formed to try to raise money for the project. Bartholdi estimated he needed $250,000 to build his monument. The original French plan had been to present the statue to the people of the United States on July 4, 1876, as a present for the nation's one hundredth birthday, but all the delays made this idea impossible.

As part of the French fund-raising campaign, a newspaper appeal was launched, a glittering banquet was held in Paris, and a special cantata, "Liberty Enlightening the World," was composed by Charles Gounod and performed at the Paris Grand Opera. Dinners and art benefits held in lavish fashion followed. Large donations poured in from 181 municipalities and from many wealthy contributors.

It was now possible for work on the statue to begin. The construction was to take place in the largest workshop Bartholdi could find in Paris—the workshop of Gaget, Gauthier and Company—which he rented in January 1876. The workers there were experienced artisans who had made the statues and spires for the top of the famous cathedral of Notre Dame in Paris. For Bartholdi's project, however, the workshop had to be enlarged.

On his first visit to Gaget, Gauthier and Company, Bartholdi brought along a four-foot model of a dignified lady draped in a classic Roman-style gown. Next to her sandaled feet lay a broken chain. The grim expression on her face and the broken chain were the sculptor's attempt to show that the lady had to fight off tyranny to achieve her freedom. Her face looked as if she had undergone and had understood suffering. On her head was a crown of seven spikes meant to represent the seven continents and seas of the world. In her upraised hand the lady carried a torch, which served to emphasize that her purpose was to enlighten the world.

Hundreds of workers including carpenters, blacksmiths, copper workers, engineers, plasterers, and other artisans listened as the sculptor outlined how he hoped work would proceed. Bartholdi explained that he had decided to use copper for the statue's "skin" because it would be light, easy to work with, and strong enough to stand up during a long ocean voyage. In addition, copper would hold up well in the salty air of New York harbor and was also cheaper than bronze or other copper alloys.

Work began by enlarging the four-foot model Bartholdi had made out of clay. Using the clay model as a guide, he began to make a second model out of plaster that would be nine feet tall.

Bartholdi asked his mother to pose for the model's face. Madame Bartholdi sat very still for two days as her son copied her stern features in wet plaster, but Bartholdi knew he needed a younger woman to take on the much more demanding job of posing for the model's body. For that job he hired his friend, Jeanne-Emilie Baheux de Puysieux, who was working in Paris as a dressmaker's helper at the time. For two weeks Jeanne-Emilie cheerfully stood on a box wearing a long gown and holding a book and a torch. She never complained of being tired during her ten-hour work days. Her chatter entertained the sculptor as he worked, and he soon found himself falling in love.

The nine-foot model was finished by the middle of February 1876. The next model, which would be thirty-six feet tall, required a scaffold and ladders and would barely fit in the workshop. Each part of the nine-foot model had to be enlarged four times. The job, however, was completed by April.

It was now time to work on the full-sized statue. The thirty-six-foot model was marked off into 300 sections, each of which was enlarged approximately four times. This was an incredibly demanding and time-consuming job because 9,000 separate measurements had to be made on every one of the 300 sections. As the statue got bigger, Bartholdi had to watch the enlarging process very carefully to make sure it remained true to his original model.

Because there was no way in which the full-sized statue could fit in the workshop, the craftsmen had to work on the statue one section at a time. They began by constructing the right arm holding the torch because Bartholdi had been asked to send that part to the United States to display at the 1876 Fourth of July centennial celebration in Philadelphia.

Madame Bartholdi, the sculptor's mother, was the model for the statue's stern face.

The carpenters were first instructed to build a tall wooden framework. To it they nailed wood strips called laths, which they bent to take the shape of the arm and torch. Other workmen then began to spread plaster over the laths, using the thirty-six-foot model as their guide to shape the full-sized arm and torch. When Bartholdi was sure the plaster was hard, he told the workmen to saw the arm and torch into twenty-one sections. The outside or "skin" side of each section was then covered with laths that were attached to heavy wooden forms. When the forms were lifted from the plaster sections, they formed hollow shells or molds.

Workmen are applying plaster to the wooden framework of Liberty's hand and arm. Note the worker completely covered with plaster.

Metal workers fit a copper sheet into a wooden mold to shape a small portion of Liberty's skin.

It was then that the noisiest work began as metal workers hammered copper sheets as thin as half dollars to fit the insides of the molds. After making sure a copper sheet was pounded to a perfect fit, the sheet was lifted out carefully and the piece of "copper skin" completed. Eventually there would be 300 copper plates, one for each plaster section.

While this work was under way, Bartholdi was also involved in trying to plan how his colossal statue could be supported. Some statues are thick enough to stand without an interior structure, but there was, of course, no way in which the thin copper sheets attached to each other could stand up by themselves, particularly in such a gigantic structure as Liberty. Since figuring out how to keep the copper-skinned lady from sagging and collapsing was beyond the knowledge of Bartholdi, he called in the engineer Emmanuel Viollet-le-Duc, who was a structural specialist, to solve the problem.

Viollet-le-Duc felt the only way to keep Liberty standing was to put something heavy in her and suggested a system of interior compartments filled with sand. Then if an accident occurred and repair work needed to be done, a valve could be opened and the sand drained out of a single compartment, giving access to one section of the interior at a time. He planned to fill Liberty with sand up to her waist, which he thought would give her plenty of ballast to withstand the winds of New York harbor. The upper body would have a lighter iron framework to which the skin would be attached. The plan was accepted, and work on the copper sections continued.

As the time for the centennial celebration neared, Bartholdi thought it would be a good idea if he accompanied the arm and torch to the United States. He wanted to make sure the people there had not forgotten his project. He left France in May 1876 before the torch and arm were finished. When he arrived, he spoke eloquently about the statue at meetings and dinners and wrote articles for newspapers and magazines.

By June the completed arm holding the torch was packed in twenty-one crates and shipped to the United States. As the result of a series of setbacks, it missed the July Fourth celebration but was displayed at the Centennial International Exhibition in Philadelphia. Later it was moved to New York, where it was set up in Madison Square at Fifth Avenue and 23rd Street as a fund-raising scheme. A visitor could pay fifty cents and climb up a steel ladder to the torch's balcony. Eventually the arm and torch were taken apart and returned to Paris so that the statue could be completed.

On September 6 Bartholdi was in New York for the unveiling of his statue of the Marquis de Lafayette. It was well received, and the occasion gave Bartholdi a good opportunity to talk about fund-raising for Liberty Enlightening the World.

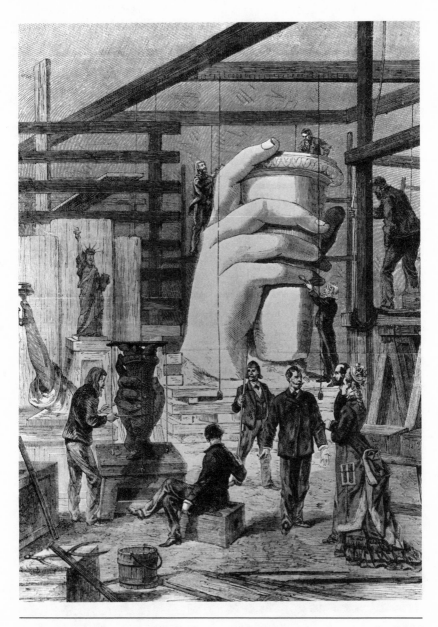

An engraving from *Le Monde* shows workmen hurrying to get the hand and torch ready to ship to the United States for display at the Centennial International Exhibition in Philadelphia.

A print that appeared in *Frank Leslie's Illustrated Newspaper* of Liberty's arm on display in Philadelphia.

During his second visit to the United States, Bartholdi missed his friend Jeanne-Emilie, and at the end of the summer he wrote asking her to come to America as soon as possible and marry him. It is said that Bartholdi had been afraid to marry Jeanne-Emilie because he was fearful of his mother's disapproval. Jeanne-Emilie was a Catholic, and her family was not wealthy, while Madame Bartholdi was a devout Protestant and had very high standards for the kind of daughter-in-law she would accept.

One story has it that Bartholdi found a clergyman in Newport who was willing to sign a paper saying Jeanne-Emilie was a Unitarian. That made her a Protestant, although it was not quite the same as being a strict Calvinist Protestant as was the formidable Madame Bartholdi. Then it was reported that she was a cousin of Margaret LaFarge, the wife of Auguste's good friend John LaFarge; such a relationship gave a considerable boost to Jeanne-Emilie's social status. Finally, on December 20, 1876, Jeanne-Emilie Baheux de Puysieux married Frédéric Auguste Bartholdi in Newport, Rhode Island. It all turned out very well, however, because sweet, friendly Jeanne-Emilie won over her mother-in-law, and the two became the best of friends.

Before returning to France on January 2, 1877, Bartholdi attended a meeting of key public leaders at the Century Association in New York City, chaired by William M. Evarts, a prominent New Yorker who later became a United States senator. In a speech the sculptor reminded his audience that it was the responsibility of the United States to pay for the pedestal and foundation of his statue.

Efforts to raise funds in the United States had not been very successful. As a result of Bartholdi's plea, the American Committee of the French-American Union was formed under the leadership of William M. Evarts to raise the $125,000 thought necessary to pay for the foundation and pedestal. As in France, the early fund-raising was directed to the wealthy, and soon enough money had been donated to start looking around for an architect to design the pedestal.

Shortly after Bartholdi's second visit to the United States, President Grant signed a resolution that formally accepted Liberty Enlightening the World as a gift from France to the United States. Congress was to "designate and set apart a site on Governor's or Bedloe's Island" and to "cause suitable regulations to be made for its future maintenance as a beacon and for the permanent care and preservation thereof as a monument of art and of the continued good will of the great nation which aided us in our struggle for freedom." The date was February 22, 1877, the anniversary of the birth of George Washington.

They were fancy words, but there was no mention of any funds to be provided by the United States to build the pedestal or maintain the statue. The fund-raising was left up to the American Committee.

During 1878 Liberty's head was displayed at the Paris Universal Exhibition. Once more a visitor for a small fee could climb into part of the statue. The money was donated to the French fund for the statue's construction.

It had become a popular pastime in Paris to take a stroll over to the workshop where Liberty was being put together. Watching the work in progress prompted many spectators to give speeches about Liberty and the country that was to be her home. Bartholdi encouraged these visits. As long as Liberty was on everyone's mind, he hoped he would have funds to finish the project. His original estimate of $250,000 was proving to be too low. It looked as if the final cost of the statue would be double that amount.

Visitors to the workshop were sometimes a little baffled by what they saw. A hand might be in one corner, a foot in another, and a string of toes in yet another. Looking around at Liberty's 300 pieces, they wondered whether a colossal massacre had occurred, but behind the confusion there was a carefully designed plan that would eventually bring order out of what looked like chaos.

Liberty's head is displayed at the Paris Universal Exhibition in 1878.

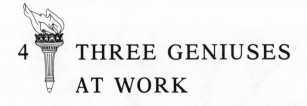

4 THREE GENIUSES AT WORK

A year after Liberty's head went on display at the Paris Universal Exhibition, the man in charge of Liberty's interior framework, Emmanuel Viollet-le-Duc, died, and the most famous engineer in all of France took over for him. Gustave Eiffel was about the same age as Bartholdi and was very much like him in personality. Both men believed there was no challenge they could not meet and conquer. Also, like Bartholdi, Eiffel had a strong, energetic mother upon whom he doted all his life.

In the late 1800s, France, like the United States, was moving into the age of railroads. Building was easier in the United States, however, because of its great stretches of flat farmland and prairies. France, on the other hand, is hilly and mountainous in many places, and there were a multitude of wide, deep ravines and rivers that the train tracks had to cross. Since the trains built in those days could manage to climb only a slight incline, a way had to be found to provide a fairly level railroad track. Hundreds of tunnels had to be cut through mountains, and bridges had to be built across rivers. Had it not been for Gustave Eiffel, the age of railroads might have been delayed in France. Eiffel's specialty became building long railroad bridges that looked light and airy but were enormously strong.

Two features of his bridges made him the perfect choice for creating Liberty's skeleton. He often built high, spidery iron towers or pylons as bases. He also had the amazing ability to design joints that were flexible enough to withstand the expansion and contraction of metal parts caused by changes in temperature and at the same time were able to take the shock of a moving train and the blasts of wind that might sweep down a mountain valley. Flexibility was also very important for the giant lady who was going to stand in the middle of New York harbor and whose extraordinary size would subject her to more wind than any sail had ever had to handle.

For her backbone, which would bear most of the weight of the statue, Eiffel designed a narrow, spidery four-legged tower or pylon tapered at the top, to be built of wrought-iron columns and crossbeams. The structure was very similar to the pylons Eiffel used for his railway bridges. The four legs of the tower would be bolted to massive beams deep in the pedestal.

Solving the problem of how the statue would be supported, however, was only one of Bartholdi's problems as the 1870s came to a close. His worst problem was that he was running out of money. The rich who had given before did not seem to be willing to contribute more money. Then in 1880 the French-American Union came up with a brilliant plan. A national lottery was held, and it was a huge success. Contributions then poured in from hundreds of thousands of people from every walk of life. One million school children donated their pennies to the fund. Building Liberty soon became a national movement.

At about the same time as Gustave Eiffel was designing the statue's interior and the lottery was being held in France, the United States got to work on the pedestal. Richard Morris Hunt, whom Bartholdi had met in Newport, was chosen to be the architect. Hunt was well known as the designer of various public buildings and of mansions for millionaires in New York and Newport, many of which were as large and elaborate as European castles. Newly rich people felt they had made it in society if they could get "Dick" Hunt to design a home for them.

Another reason for choosing Richard Morris Hunt was his devotion to France and to French republican ideas. He had received his architectural training in France and was the first American to graduate from the École des Beaux Arts in Paris.

There was a great deal of discussion and argument about the height of the pedestal. It could not be so tall that the statue, which was 151 feet, 1 inch, from base to torch, would look small by comparison. On the other hand, it would not do to have Liberty on a stumpy pedestal where she would scarcely be noticed from Manhattan or by ships entering the harbor. Hunt's first design was massive and rose 114 feet from its foundation. It was finally decided that 89 feet would be an ideal height.

General Charles P. Stone, a Civil War veteran, was the engineer chosen to oversee the construction of the foundation and pedestal. He was a fortunate choice because, like Eiffel, Stone was a brilliant, creative engineer. It was his decision to make the foundation and pedestal out of poured concrete, and it was to be by far the largest single concrete mass of its time.

Bedloe's Island contained the remains of an old star-shaped fort named Fort Wood built in the early 1800s to defend the harbor during the War of 1812. Along the outside battery were several rusty cannons. On one side was an arched entrance, as well as a trench, which probably had been a moat. There was even a place that appeared to have been set up for a drawbridge.

Within the walls of the fort were an open space, which was probably used for a parade ground, and a couple of houses for men and officers. Also, as in castles of old, there were huge tanks for storing water and enormous storerooms and vaults.

It was decided that the monument should be erected within the walls of the fort. The big problem, however, was that the parade ground was made of sand. Since it would not do to place the heavy statue on such a precarious base, excavations had to be made to get to firmer ground. General Stone gave the order to start digging. Very soon the going became very difficult because the workmen ran into massive brick and stone walls built to protect the water tanks, underground storerooms, and vaults. A pit was finally dug that was 91 feet square. The bottom was almost solid rock 13 feet above sea level.

The great pit now had to be filled with wet concrete, which was a mixture of cement, broken stones, and water. It was poured

Gustave Eiffel

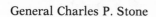

General Charles P. Stone

into place one layer at a time, which the workmen had to beat down and smooth out. When it became as hard as rock, another layer was added. When finished, the concrete mass rose to the broad walk of the walls of the fort.

The foundation ended up as a huge tapering block of concrete that was 53 feet deep, 91 feet square at the bottom, and 65 feet square at the top. Over the foundation Stone planned to place the pedestal, which would be 65 feet wide at the bottom, where it joined the foundation, and 43 feet wide at the top, where the statue was to stand. There would be a central opening of 27 square feet in the top of the pedestal to permit entry into the statue. The massive walls of the pedestal were to be 8 to 19 feet in thickness and were also to be made from poured concrete. Only the outside decorative portions were to be made of granite brought from a Connecticut stone quarry.

While construction of the foundation and the pedestal began on Bedloe's Island, across the ocean the pieces of Liberty were put together on the street outside the Paris workshop. The giant pylon or primary framework serving as Liberty's backbone was built first. Planning the rest of Liberty's skeleton, however, created engineering problems that would not arise again until men began building skyscrapers. For Viollet-le-Duc, the solution for keeping such a tall structure standing was great weight. For Gustave Eiffel, the answer lay in the opposite direction. For the greatest possible flexibility, he wanted to keep the statue as light as possible. Of course, the interior framework also had to be strong enough to support the weight of the huge statue.

His plan was to surround the central pylon with an envelope of horizontal and vertical bars that roughly formed the shape of the statue. This was called the secondary frame. Flat, spring-like iron bars were attached to the secondary frame, which projected outward and upward. At its far end each bar was attached by a single bolt to a shaped rib that followed the contours of the copper skin.

Next came the most brilliant part of the design. The ribs were not fastened directly to the copper but passed through U-shaped fittings, or saddles, riveted to the inside of the skin, thus making

Outside the Paris workshop, Liberty's central pylon is surrounded by the secondary framework.

it possible for the skin to slide up and down and to move freely. It could expand and contract with changes in temperature and would respond safely to the pressure of wind. In effect, the skin of Liberty would be able to "breathe." This method of stressed skin construction was probably invented by Eiffel and later would be used for making aircraft wings and for what was to be called curtain walls in skyscrapers.

Huge crowds came to watch every day as the copper plates, one by one, were carried out of the workshop and attached from the ground up. By the time the statue was completed, there were approximately 1,500 copper saddles that linked 600 vertical and 750 horizontal ribs to the fragile copper skin. Each rib had to be custom-made to fit exactly into the intricate contours of robe, torch, face, arms, feet, fingers, and toes. Engineers called this arrangement of ribs and saddles the "armature."

Eiffel had another difficult problem to solve. He knew that when certain kinds of metals are pressed together, a conductor, which could be as simple as moisture in the air, can make the two metals act like a battery. Electric currents begin to flow between them. This process gradually corrodes one of the metals.

Copper and iron happen to be two metals that are not compatible. Iron is the inferior metal and will begin to rust and crumble if placed in direct contact with copper in the presence of a conductor. There was an enormous amount of iron right next to the copper in the statue. To protect the iron ribs from the copper saddles, Eiffel ordered that asbestos strips soaked in shellac be carefully inserted in every place where the saddles would touch the ribs. Thinking that he had solved the problem of this destructive electrochemical process known as galvanic action was to be Gustave Eiffel's greatest and perhaps only major engineering mistake.

Piece by piece Liberty took shape. Finally, in early 1884, she stood completed in a Paris street towering over nearby buildings. On July 4 of that same year she was formally presented to the United States during a ceremony attended by the American Minister to France. At this point, back in the United States, the foundation was just up to the level of the old parade ground.

The copper skin is attached from the bottom up as the completed head and arm with torch wait to be fitted on last of all.

Liberty stands completed in a Paris street.

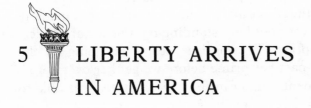

5 LIBERTY ARRIVES IN AMERICA

In the United States, actual work on the pedestal had yet to begin, but the cost had almost doubled from the original estimate of $125,000. Yet raising more funds was proving to be increasingly difficult if not impossible. There seemed to be much more enthusiasm for building monuments in France than there was in the United States at that time. In addition, many patrons of the arts in this country did not think much of Liberty as a work of art.

It was really not exactly clear to many people what the statue represented. Some saw her as a "pagan goddess." Some wealthy people saw her as a fire-carrying revolutionary whose purpose was to lead the oppressed poor to overthrow the government as had been done in the French Revolution. To avoid this image, Bartholdi had specifically made Liberty as dignified and ladylike as possible. Still the idea of a huge lady in the harbor carrying a torch made some Americans a little nervous.

Various segments of the population felt contributing was no concern of theirs. The poor felt it was a pet project of the wealthy. People living outside of New York City felt that since the statue was to be in New York harbor, New Yorkers ought to pay for it. New Yorkers resented having to bear the cost alone. Still others said that if the statue was a gift from France, the French should then pay for the whole thing.

The debate about financing the pedestal was heatedly discussed in the country's newspapers. Often cartoons were printed that poked fun at the whole affair. One cartoon that ran in many papers showed a very old lady standing on a pedestal. Underneath ran the caption: "If America doesn't get going on the pedestal she'll be past her prime before we get her over here."

At last one influential man in the United States was able to overcome the indifference of the American people toward the French gift. Joseph Pulitzer was a Hungarian immigrant who served in the Union Army during the Civil War and later became active in politics in St. Louis. In 1878 he became owner of a newspaper there, and in 1883 he bought *The World*, a New York paper.

That same year Pulitzer ran editorials in *The World* attacking the wealthy for not supporting the Liberty project. Pulitzer's interest in promoting the statue was twofold. He was genuinely angered at America's apathetic attitude, but he also hoped a fund-raising campaign would boost his paper's circulation.

One of Pulitzer's ideas was to hold a poetry contest. A quiet, intellectual young New York poet and essayist named Emma Lazarus was encouraged to write a poem to submit to the contest. At first she did not want to do it. She did not like the idea of writing poetry to raise money, but she was stirred to participate by something that was happening in Russia.

Two years earlier Czar Alexander II had been assassinated by Russian revolutionaries. His death set off a series of violent anti-Semitic riots in Russia. Emma Lazarus was a member of New York's Sephardic Jewish community. She felt enormous sympathy for the hundreds of thousands of Jews who were persecuted and had to flee the country. These events awoke in her a new awareness of her heritage, and she tried to comfort forlorn refugees pouring into New York by writing the following poem she called "The New Colossus":

Not like the brazen giant of Greek fame,
With conquering limbs astride from land to land;
Here at our sea-washed, sunset gates shall stand
A mighty woman with a torch, whose flame

Joseph Pulitzer

Emma Lazarus

Is the imprisoned lightning, and her name
Mother of Exiles. From her beacon-hand
Glows world-wide welcome; her mild eyes command
The air-bridged harbor that twin cities frame.
"Keep, ancient lands, your storied pomp!" cries she
With silent lips. "Give me your tired, your poor,
Your huddled masses yearning to breathe free,
The wretched refuse of your teeming shore.
Send these, the homeless, tempest-tost to me.
I lift my lamp beside the golden door!"

At the time it was published, the poem went almost unnoticed. Later, however, it would be an important factor in changing the image of the statue from Liberty Enlightening the World to the Mother of Exiles.

Pulitzer's 1883 appeal seemed to fall on deaf ears. Despite the fact that the pedestal was not finished and fund-raising was disappointing, in January 1885 the statue, still standing on display in the Paris street, was closed to the public and the work of disassembling was begun. The workers numbered parts and sections before placing them carefully in 214 crates. Then, Pulitzer once again campaigned to raise funds to complete the pedestal. This time he was very successful in convincing the American people that they should be grateful for the gift from the French and that it was everybody's duty to help pay for it.

The key to Pulitzer's success was that he published the names of every single donor even if they gave as little as ten cents to the cause. Along with names he published colorful letters from the gift-givers. Many of the letters chided the rich for not being more generous. One contributor wrote saying, "I have lost 25 pounds and I am happily sending in a penny per pound. May heaven help you in your good work. It seems that New York's rich men do not."

As in France, the final drive for funds for the statue in the United States became a movement of the people. The cause also attracted the attention of school children all over the country, and they began sending their pennies or whatever they had to give. One letter printed in *The World* came from a young reader living in Metuchen, New Jersey. In it she said, "I am a little girl, nine years old, and would like to do something for the Statue Fund. I will send you a pair of my pet game bantams if you will sell them and give the money to the Statue."

As the money dribbled in and then began to pour in for completing the pedestal, preparations for moving the statue from Paris to New York began on the other side of the Atlantic in the spring of 1885.

After being packed for four months, the 214 crates were loaded onto 17 railroad cars and transported from Paris to the river

The cover engraving of *L'Illustration* shows a joyous celebration taking place in New York harbor as the French transport *Isère* arrives on June 17, 1885, loaded with the crated parts of Liberty. The people in the foreground are viewing the scene from the uncompleted pedestal.

port of Rouen. There they were put aboard the *Isère*, a French navy transport, which sailed for the United States on May 21, 1885. During the crossing the ship was battered by a fierce North Atlantic storm. On June 17 she arrived off Sandy Hook, and the French North Atlantic Naval Squadron proudly escorted the *Isère* into New York harbor. The next day the crates were unloaded on Bedloe's Island as thousands of spectators looked on from ferries in the harbor.

The World now increased its fund-raising efforts, and on August 11, 1885, the following headline appeared in the paper: ONE HUNDRED THOUSAND DOLLARS! TRIUMPHANT COMPLETION OF THE WORLD'S FUND FOR THE LIBERTY PEDESTAL. The money had been raised by a multitude of small contributions from the people, with the average donation being less than a dollar!

From stories like those printed in *The World*, the myth grew that the pedestal was paid for by American school children. It was also said the statue itself was paid for by French school children. The truth is that people rich and poor, young and old, American and French, all contributed to the Statue of Liberty. She therefore belonged to a lot of people because a great many people in both countries helped pay for her.

Work continued on the pedestal, and on November 4, 1885, Auguste Bartholdi arrived to help Charles Stone with final plans for mounting the statue on her stand. The sculptor stayed for only three weeks before returning home, leaving the actual work of putting Liberty together in American hands.

First of all, four steel girders were planted horizontally deep within the interior walls of the pedestal to form a square. A similar square was placed a few feet from the top of the pedestal. The two squares were connected by iron beams, which also extended into the statue's skeleton. This arrangement gave the statue a tremendously firm base support. Next, the primary structure or pylon was erected on the pedestal and the secondary structure added.

As the statue rose to its full height, problems began to develop. Even though some of the workers were members of the French

An engraving from the French newspaper *Journal Universel* shows work-men looking like tiny insects as they labor dangerously high in the air to attach Liberty's copper skin plates to her iron framework.

crew, they had trouble fitting together both the interior framework and the outer skin. Workers had to dangle precariously high over the windswept harbor trying to fit the pieces together. It was like working on a huge jigsaw puzzle, and it is not surprising that a few mistakes were made.

For some reason the workers did not place the head squarely over the pylon. The upheld arm was also put on too much to the side. As a result, Liberty's head and arm were attached about two feet to the right of where Eiffel's drawings showed he wanted them. The mistake weakened the arm because its weight was not carried directly to the pylon.

There were more problems when it came time to attach the 300 copper-skin plates. Many parts did not fit quite right. Perhaps the copper plates, which had been piled on top of each other for many months, might have flattened slightly under their own weight. The sheets might also have expanded somewhat from the summer's heat. At any rate, whenever the workers on the scaffolds could not fit the pieces together, they drilled new rivet holes, leaving Liberty sprinkled with thousands of original and unused rivet holes open to the weather. In all, 600,000 rivets bound the copper skin to the saddles, through which the iron ribs passed in the statue's interior. At each place where copper touched iron, pieces of asbestos soaked in shellac were inserted to prevent corrosion as Gustave Eiffel had instructed.

Toward the end of the summer of 1886, the end was in sight. A huge dedication ceremony was planned for October 28, 1886, but once again lack of funds became a problem. Finally Senator William M. Evarts persuaded President Cleveland and Congress to appropriate $60,000 to pay for the dedication ceremonies and for the maintenance of the statue as a lighthouse. There was no restriction put on the appropriation except that no part of the money was to be spent for refreshments at the dedication ceremony.

The only problem with designating the statue as a lighthouse was that Liberty had no light in her torch. Electric lights had not yet been invented when Bartholdi designed his statue. The

A print that appeared in *Frank Leslie's Illustrated Newspaper* showing workers inside Liberty's head attaching the copper skin to the saddles through which the ribs are passed.

original torch had solid copper sheeting that Bartholdi hoped would one day be gilded.

It is true that Bartholdi had envisioned Liberty to serve as a lighthouse and had planned for lookouts to patrol the small balcony around the torch and report any problems taking place on ships entering or leaving the harbor. He had also given instructions that a kerosene lamp be placed on the balcony.

But several years had now passed since Bartholdi designed the statue, and the light bulb had in the interim made a big impact in America. It was therefore felt that if Liberty was to serve as a lighthouse, she must be electrified.

The dedication was fast approaching. Federal money could be used for an electric light plant, but the funds had not yet been delivered. At the very last minute, a private company, the American Electric Manufacturing Company, donated an electric power plant. Two horizontal rows of circular holes were cut in the flame. Each of these holes was covered by a round piece of glass plate so the lights placed inside could shine through.

At long last the big day arrived. A French delegation including Bartholdi, Ferdinand de Lesseps, the chairman of the French-American Union, and their wives were on hand for the ceremonies. Édouard de Laboulaye had died a few years earlier, and Bartholdi's mother thought she was too old and ill to make the trip.

October 28, 1886, was given the official name of "Bartholdi Day." Unfortunately, the weather was raw and rainy, but it did not seem to dampen anyone's enthusiasm. New Yorkers went wild over the Statue of Liberty.

Along the five-mile parade route a million people vigorously waving flags of both the United States and France watched the biggest parade in the city's history. Twenty thousand members of the armed forces, veterans of the Grand Army of the Republic, bands, patriotic societies, and school groups marched from 57th Street to the Battery. Important dignitaries viewing the parade had to call off their official luncheon because the parade went on for much longer than anyone expected. After it ended, the

VIPs had to rush over to the East River in order to get on boats to view a naval parade proceeding down the harbor.

The crowds who followed the parade down to the Battery could barely see the Statue of Liberty through the rain. The ordinary people who had helped pay for the pedestal were left standing on the shore as people began to board the official boats going to the dedication ceremony. Space on Bedloe's Island was, of course, limited. Some of the privileged few aboard the boats had worked hard for Liberty. Others were influential, rich people who had done nothing for the monument but had talked their way into taking part in the dedication festivities.

Only two women were invited to the ceremony—Jeanne-Emilie Bartholdi and Tototte de Lesseps. The official reason given for not inviting more women was they might get injured in the crowd on the small island, but the truth was at that time women were not often invited to important ceremonies.

Women were just then beginning to protest their not being given the same opportunities as men and had begun to fight for their rights in what was called the Woman Suffrage Movement. Mainly they wanted the right to vote. On the day of Liberty's unveiling a group of suffragettes chartered a boat and closely circled Bedloe's Island. There were no electronic loudspeakers, so the women had to shout as loudly as possible in order to be heard on the island. The speakers on the island, of course, also had to shout to be heard above the racket taking place in the harbor. There was one woman aboard who seemed to have a more powerful voice than any of the male speakers at the ceremony. She shouted how wonderful it was that the Statue of Liberty was a woman and what a terrible shame it would be if Liberty came to life and would be unable to vote in the United States or France.

Bartholdi crouched in the crown of the statue waiting for a signal to pull the rope holding in place the flag covering the statue's face. Because of the dense fog and the general confusion, it was difficult for him to see and hear what was going on below.

During a somewhat long-winded speech by Senator Evarts,

Bartholdi mistakenly thought the signal had been given, and he released the flag. The speech was forgotten as a tumult of cheers, boat whistles, foghorns, and firing guns greeted the unveiling. Evarts put his hands to his ears and sat down.

When things quieted down, President Cleveland, who had repeatedly refused to allocate funds for the statue, gave a very moving speech in which he said:

> We will not forget that Liberty has made here her home, nor shall her chosen altar be neglected. Willing voteries will constantly keep alive its fires and these shall gleam upon the shores of our sister republic in the east. Reflected thence and joined with answering rays, a stream of light shall pierce the darkness of ignorance and man's oppression until Liberty enlightens the world.

It was probably the finest day of Auguste Bartholdi's whole life. He announced happily that his great dream had come true. He had created a colossal symbol of unity and friendship between two nations—two great republics. He also remarked proudly, "It is a consolation to know that this statue will exist thousands of years from now, long after our names shall have been forgotten." Bartholdi envisioned the statue standing as long as the great pyramids of Egypt. What he did not realize was that, based in New York harbor next to the world's second largest city, Liberty had to face more difficult conditions than the pyramids standing in the middle of an Egyptian desert.

Guns are fired as Liberty is unveiled on her dedication day, October 28, 1886, as shown in a painting by Edward Moran.

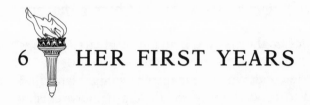

6 HER FIRST YEARS

The Statue of Liberty was a pretty impressive sight to the citizens of New York. She was higher than the towers of the newly built Brooklyn Bridge, and she was also taller than the highest building in New York City, which happened to be Trinity Church, which won that distinction by virtue of its steeple.

There was considerable speculation at the time about whether or not such a colossal structure could survive in such an unprotected setting. A group of citizens decided there were five dangers to be feared—earthquakes, wind, lightning, galvanic action, and man.

Being of a practical nature, they decided that in the unlikely event an earthquake occurred, the whole city would be destroyed and so nobody would notice if the statue toppled over. Carefully looking at the construction of the statue, they decided that the shocks of heavy winds had been considered and provided for in a brilliant fashion by virtue of the flexibility of the structure. The statue had also been satisfactorily equipped with lightning protection.

Judging from past events in history, they agreed it was entirely possible that some day man might pull down the statue or that an enemy fleet might use it as a target. They all also agreed that there was no way to avoid such a fate. It would not be practical, desirable, or artistic to surround Liberty with shellproof armor.

The scientific experts were in total agreement that there was no need to fear galvanic action. They were sure Eiffel's ingenious use of asbestos soaked with shellac would forever keep the copper from coming into contact with the iron framework. How wrong they were!

Since nothing further could be done to protect Liberty from natural and man-made disasters, concern for and interest in the statue soon diminished. New Yorkers returned to their hectic everyday lives.

Things were pretty quiet, therefore, on Bedloe's Island as Liberty began her first century there. The island itself, however, had already had quite a history.

When the early explorers arrived, Bedloe's Island belonged to the Mohegan Indians, who were also called the Monatons or Manhattans. The English seized the island from the Indians in 1664. At that time they called it Oyster Island, presumably because the surrounding waters abounded in shellfish. In 1668 the island was sold to a wealthy merchant of New Amsterdam named Issack Bedloo, who regarded it as a very special place and renamed it Love Island. Five years later Issack Bedloo died, and his widow eventually sold the island.

After passing through a series of owners, the island was bought by Captain Archibald Kennedy, who was the commander of the British naval station in New York. He built a house there and used the island as a summer residence, and for a time the island was known as Kennedy's Island. It was Mr. Bedloo's name, however, that seemed to become attached to the island, although the spelling changed from "Bedloo" to "Bedlow" and finally to "Bedloe."

Captain Kennedy occasionally rented his island. On July 9, 1753, he ran this advertisement in *The New York Gazette:*

> To be let: Bedloe's Island, alias Love Island, together with the Dwelling House and Light House, being finely situated for a tavern, where all kinds of garden stuff, poultry, &c. may be easily raised for the shipping outward bound, and from where any quantity of pickled oysters may be transported; it abounds with English Rabbits.

Oyster feasts were very popular at that time. These delectable shellfish were so plentiful in the harbor that anyone could afford

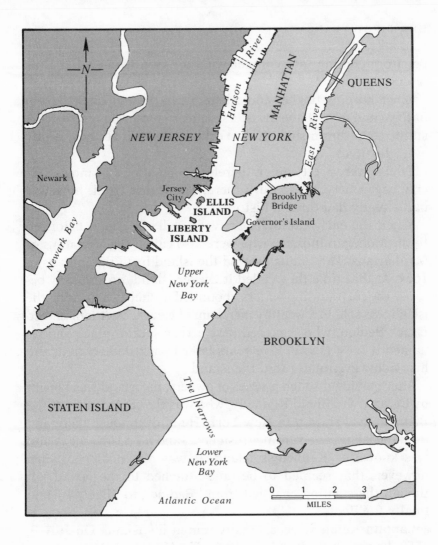

to buy them. Many parties enjoyed coming out to Bedloe's Island to gather and feast on oysters. Those they didn't eat at once they preserved by pickling.

Finally in 1759 Captain Kennedy decided to sell his island. It was a wise decision because as commander of the British Navy in the harbor during the American Revolution, he would have undoubtedly lost it following the war.

Both New York and New Jersey were interested in purchasing

the island. Since it lay closer to New Jersey than to New York, by rights it should have belonged to New Jersey. New York, however, worked out an arrangement whereby it would buy the island and New Jersey would get the rights to the water around it. Owning the oyster beds may have been helpful in getting New Jersey to agree to this arrangement. Later, New Jersey was to regret giving up Bedloe's Island, which is what it continued to be called.

After purchasing the island, New York built a hospital there and used it as a quarantine station. New York City was growing quickly, and since not much was known about sanitation in those days, people often became ill with diseases for which doctors had no cure. There was a fear of epidemics, particularly yellow fever, so when citizens got sick with something thought to be contagious, they were packed off to places like Bedloe's Island until they got better—or died.

During the American Revolution Bedloe's Island was captured by the British. The patriots then raided it and burned most of the buildings. After the war the island was once again used as a quarantine station, but between epidemics it was leased to citizens who probably went back to gathering and pickling oysters.

For the three years from 1793 and 1796, New York lent the island to the French fleet to use as an isolation station and a hospital.

At the turn of the century, on February 15, 1800, the New York legislature ceded Bedloe's Island and nearby Ellis and Governor's islands to the United States government for defense purposes. Between 1806 to 1811 a fort in the shape of an eleven-pointed star was erected at one end of the island. The fort, known as Fort Wood, was manned during the War of 1812.

The next seventy years were years of unprecedented peace. Bedloe's Island continued to be a military garrison but was increasingly inactive. The United States Army was still in charge of the island when Liberty arrived and continued to stay on after she was erected. Bartholdi envisioned elaborate landscap-

Army housing on Bedloe's Island in 1864

ing around the statue, but this was not possible so long as the island was filled with rundown army barracks and an abandoned hospital.

The story of the Statue of Liberty in her first years in the United States was largely a story of confusion and neglect. The United States government had somewhat reluctantly accepted the statue as a gift from France, but it had not really decided whether to treat her as an aid to navigation, as a monument, or as art. There was also a question as to whether Congress had an obligation to protect and maintain the colossal lady.

Ten years earlier President Grant had signed a resolution accepting the gift from France as a beacon. For lack of a better plan, it was finally decided that Liberty would be primarily a lighthouse. On November 16, 1886, a month after the dedication ceremony, President Cleveland signed an order that placed the statue "under the care of superintendance of the Lighthouse Board" and that "it be from henceforth maintained by said Board as a beacon."

In early 1887 one acre in the northwest part of the military reservation was set aside as a lighthouse reserve. A tumbledown, abandoned hospital building was fixed up as a residence for the lightkeeper.

The only problem was that Liberty never worked very well as a lighthouse. When the electric light was turned on for the first time the night of the dedication, the beam had been disappointingly weak. The statue's fourteen-arc lamp powered by a steam dynamo was not very strong, and also the torch was too high to be effective as a lighthouse beacon. As a lighthouse, Liberty was a flop.

Although she continued to be operated and maintained by the Lighthouse Board, actually using her as an aid to navigation was quickly abandoned. Small improvements were made in the lighting system, but they were made mostly for decorative reasons. Liberty in her childhood was far from lavishly maintained. Her annual expenses for 1887, including the salaries for those taking care of her, were $7,500.

Most confusing was that Liberty had too many parents. The Lighthouse Board was officially in charge of the light and to some extent of the statue itself. But her island belonged to the United States Army, which made her their responsibility, too. The Citizens Committee in New York, which took over for the French-American Committee, was in charge of the tourist business to the island, arranging for sightseeing ferries and visits inside the statue. Therefore, with no one agency clearly in charge, Liberty was often sadly neglected.

During this time one of her visitors was Bartholdi himself. He came often, and naturally he was disappointed when he saw what was going on at Bedloe's Island. In an 1890 interview with *The World*, he tried to inspire Americans to do something about the island he called "Liberty Island." He said, "Liberty Island is obviously destined to be made into a pleasure ground for the soul of the American people, a place of pilgrimage for citizens of the whole nation, a National museum of the glories and memories of the United States."

Sadly, few citizens of the United States shared Bartholdi's desire to landscape Liberty's island. Congressmen, too, had other matters that they considered more important.

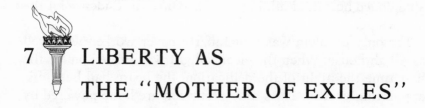

7 LIBERTY AS THE "MOTHER OF EXILES"

Liberty was soon to play an important role in one big problem the United States was facing in the late 1800s. But in order to understand the problem, it is necessary to go back a few years and examine the history of immigrants coming to America, particularly during the peak years when the flood of newcomers was almost too much for the port city of New York to handle.

The United States is a nation of immigrants. Before the American Revolution, in what is referred to as the "old" period, most settlers came from England, Scotland, Ireland, Germany, and France. A little later they began to come from Scandinavia and China as well. A sad chapter in America's history has to do with the millions of blacks brought here during this time as slaves from Africa.

Toward the end of the nineteenth century the flow of immigrants increased substantially in number. In fact, no country in the history of the modern world has ever had to deal with so many new people arriving at its shores at one time. During this period of "new" immigration, the people arrived mostly from Italy, central Europe, and Russia.

The flood of people came for many different reasons. The chief one was to escape poverty and overpopulation. Many had heard exaggerated stories of the wealth to be found in the United States. In America they felt they would not always have to be poor; there was a chance they might strike it rich.

An immigrant family

Immigrants also came to America to escape persecution. In Colonial times, settlers came to escape religious persecution. In the nineteenth century, many Germans fled from oppressive regimes and Russian Jews from Czarist pogroms. In America there was a unique opportunity to enjoy freedom of religion and speech.

For a long time it was possible for anyone to come to the New World, but as the number of immigrants continued to grow at an alarming rate, it was at last decided something had to be done to control and even limit the number of new citizens allowed into the country.

At first it was the states who had to deal with the problem by setting up their own immigration laws. People arriving had to pass through immigration centers. The insane, convicts, and people not capable of earning a living were not allowed into the country.

In 1855 a forbidding, abandoned circular fort, Fort Clinton, in lower Manhattan, which was renamed Castle Garden, was turned into New York's immigration depot. Getting in and out of Castle Garden was a frightening and often dangerous experience for the thousands of immigrants who arrived every day. Not only did they have to cope with a new language and a strange land, but they also had to deal with officials who were often corrupt and tried to take advantage of the newcomers.

The state centers for immigration became known as Dens of Thieves. A common practice was for a group of people known as runners to come into the centers as the immigrants arrived. The runners would steal goods and small children and take them to expensive boarding houses. The immigrants would be told of the thefts and had to pay ransoms to have their goods and children returned to them.

Castle Garden processed more immigrants than any other center in the country and was probably the most dangerous place of entry. In its thirty-five years of operation, more than eight million immigrants suffered indignities there before being accepted or rejected as United States citizens.

The immigration process finally became so corrupt that the federal government decided to take over. The first thing it did was to announce that Castle Garden would be closed as of April 1890. Next government officials began a search for a new immigrant landing depot. They wanted to locate it on an island in New York harbor so they could get away from the runners.

On February 28, 1890, Secretary of the Treasury Windom announced the new immigration center would be on Bedloe's Island. Once again Joseph Pulitzer came to Liberty's rescue. In a series of angry and persuasive articles in The World, he said that Bedloe's Island had been set aside exclusively for the Statue of Liberty by law and should not be used for any other purpose. He shared Bartholdi's hope that the island would one day be beautifully landscaped. Pulitzer went on to say that the federal government had been shamefully indifferent to the great monument. He stated that the only thing the government did for Liberty was to light her torch.

Pulitzer's campaign was so relentless that the federal government finally gave in and decided to build the new depot on Ellis Island. Almost two years later, on January 1, 1892, the new immigration center with its impressive red-brick buildings opened. Twenty-five hundred persons passed through the first day.

Most of the immigrants who came to the United States had very little money. They probably paid a total of about nine dollars a person for the privilege of living beneath the decks in the crowded, windowless, almost airless space called steerage. For the voyage, which lasted for more than two weeks, they lay crowded in narrow bunk beds. The smell of unbathed bodies, people getting sick, and spoiled food must have been overwhelming. While lying there, they must also have worried about their uncertain futures.

This picture of the steerage deck shows how crowded it was aboard the immigrant ships during the Atlantic crossing.

It was an exciting moment when the immigrants first saw the Statue of Liberty welcoming them to a new land.

It had to have been a great relief and a very exciting moment when their ship finally entered the Narrows and came into New York harbor. They could see hundreds of steamships at anchor flying flags from many different countries. They could begin to pick out church spires and settlements on Staten Island, New Jersey, lower Manhattan, and Brooklyn.

As they rounded the Battery, the immigrants gathered at the rail eager for their first glimpse of the lady with the torch. After a long and difficult sea voyage, Liberty stood there like a strong, giant mother welcoming her children to their new home. Tears of happiness streamed from the eyes of many of the immigrants.

The ships usually docked at one of the Hudson River piers in lower Manhattan. The well-to-do immigrants, who were first-class and cabin-class passengers, got off first and passed quickly through customs and immigration. Next, the steerage passengers got off and were put on ferries that took them to Ellis Island.

The sight of the Statue of Liberty filled the immigrants with hope, but the sight of Ellis Island filled them with dread. It was there their fate would be decided—whether or not they would be allowed to enter the United States.

Moving the immigration depot to Ellis Island had gotten rid of the runners, but unfortunately many of the same officials

---

Steerage passengers are ferried from Manhattan to Ellis Island to pass through customs and immigration.

The main immigration building on Ellis Island

who had operated Castle Garden came out to work at Ellis Island. The immigrants, coping with bundles, baggage, and children, were greeted by strange shouts and by orders and shoves by the guards. Numbered tags were pinned to their chests, and they were all herded into a huge room called the Baggage Room. There the immigrants were given the choice of checking their luggage or keeping it with them. If they chose to check it, they were told to list quickly just a few of the items checked. When they returned to reclaim their luggage, they were given only the items listed.

From the Baggage Room they moved into an open, larger, grander room known as the Great Hall. Beautiful chandeliers hung overhead. Many of the immigrants had never seen electric lights—or something even stranger, a flush toilet. They must have been overwhelmed by the size of the room and the elegance of their surroundings and must have been convinced that America was indeed a rich place.

Around the Great Hall ran a balcony, from which they were observed by medical inspectors who were trained to glance briefly at the immigrants to spot any who were not considered to be healthy. They were marked with a piece of chalk and with no explanation were put in a pen on one side of the room.

Some were marked with an "L" for lameness. If they were breathing heavily or if they were flushed, they might have been

Immigrants await their fate in the Great Hall on Ellis Island.

marked with an "H" for heart disease. If they were scratching their eyes or their eyes were runny or red, they would be marked with an "E." If they coughed, they might receive a "TB" for tuberculosis. If they were scratching their scalp, they might have received an "F" for a scalp disease called "favis."

All the immigrants who passed the medical exam were required to take a legal test. At this time they had to answer thirty questions. If they did not speak English, they were given an interpreter. Sometimes, however, the interpreters spoke in dialects strange to the immigrants.

Some of the questions were: What is your name? What is your country of origin? Are you traveling alone or are you with your family? Do you have anybody here in America who can help you find a job and a place to live? Who paid for your passage? Do you have any money? Do you have a job waiting for you in America?

This last question was a little tricky. Most immigrants did not know that it was against the law to have a job waiting unless it was supplied by a member of their family. If the answer was "yes," the immigrant had broken the law. If the answer was "no," the immigrant had to have a good reason to believe he or she could find a job.

About 20 percent of the people in the Great Hall were detained for one reason or another. They were sent to rooms upstairs. Families were split up. The men and boys stayed on one side of the building and the women and girls on the other side. During the day and evening they could gather together in the library or dining room.

The people who ran the food concession were frequently corrupt. The immigrants ate very poorly. They might receive weak soup, coffee, stewed prunes, or stale bread. Dishes and eating utensils were dirty and the floors unswept.

Immigrants were often detained for as long as four or five days while they were questioned further or examined by doctors in the island hospital. In the end only about 2 percent were sent home. It doesn't sound like a large percentage, but a total of a quarter of a million people were eventually sent back across the ocean from Ellis Island.

A child who was twelve years old was considered an adult. If a twelve-year-old failed an exam, he or she was sent back alone. The steamship companies had to pay the return fares because they should not have issued tickets to unfit immigrants. Their responsibility ended, however, with the return of an immigrant to the port where he or she boarded the ship. A twelve-year-old might be left in a port in Germany and have to make his or her way back to, for example, a small village in Poland hundreds of miles away.

An eleven-year-old who was rejected would have been a little bit luckier. One of the child's parents or an adult would have been paid to go back with the child. Many parents had to make the heartbreaking decision as to whether the father or mother should return, and it was no wonder the nickname for Ellis Island became "The Island of Tears." For those who passed

Immigrant children

through successfully, however, Ellis Island became known as
"The Golden Door" because they were given the opportunity to
start a new life in America.

At the end of the Great Hall was a door with a sign on it that
read, *"Push to New York."* It was with a feeling of enormous
relief that the accepted immigrants pushed the door open and
made their way to the last small rooms preparatory to getting
on ferries to New York.

The most corrupt officials of all probably worked in the Money
Exchange Room. The immigrants did not know how much
American money they should receive in exchange for their foreign currency. Many times they received only 25 percent of the
real value of their precious money. Worse yet, they might not
even get American money in the exchange. Instead, they might
be given gum wrappers, candy wrappers, poker chips, or even
bottle caps.

Even if the immigrants suspected they were being cheated,
there was nothing they could do about it. The officials were
dressed in soldier-like uniforms, and in Europe one did not dare
try to get a soldier in trouble. Anyway, immigrants did not want
to do anything that would risk their entry into the United States.

Down the hall from the Money Exchange Room was a post
office. Each immigrant was given a free post card to send to
relatives in the United States telling them of the person's arrival
and possibly about what train to meet.

The railroad area on Ellis Island was next to the post office.
The officials there were often corrupt, too. Immigrants wanting
to go to Chicago might be sold tickets that took them there in
a round-about way through Florida or Texas.

Many mistakes made at the railroad area, however, were not
made on purpose but were the result of language or memory
problems. Immigrants, tired after a long and confusing journey,
could not pronounce or remember names of towns and cities
where they wanted to go.

One man who hoped to find his relatives on nearby Houston
Street in New York City ended up spending thirty years of his

Immigrants, lucky enough to pass through immigration, wait for ferries to take them to Manhattan.

life in Houston, Texas. When in later years he finally visited New York City, he was glad the error had been made.

After they boarded the ferries that finally took them to Manhattan, most immigrants paused to take one last look at the lady who had welcomed them to the New World. Years later they would tell stories of their arrival in America to their children and to their grandchildren.

As the country moved into the early 1900s, Liberty was beginning to acquire a powerful, new identity. A failure as a lighthouse, the lady in the harbor became a huge success as a greeter of newcomers to the United States. Liberty Enlightening the World was assuming the role set down for her by the poet Emma Lazarus. She was truly becoming the "Mother of Exiles."

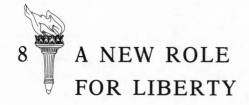

8 A NEW ROLE
FOR LIBERTY

While Liberty was a most impressive sight to immigrants viewing her from aboard ship, a closer look showed the lady needed better care than she was getting. No one noticed this more than Major A. C. Taylor, who as post commander at Ford Wood lived at Liberty's feet.

The problem, as he saw it, was the same one that had plagued the statue since her dedication. There was not sufficient interest in Liberty by government or private groups.

The Lighthouse Board found her unacceptable as a lighthouse. The thousands of immigrants for whom Liberty meant so much as they entered New York harbor ignored her as they began the struggle to begin new lives. Everybody in America seemed to be too busy to think very much about the Statue of Liberty—or to pay her a visit. As a result, the Citizens Committee did not take in much money to spend on Liberty, and what they did earn did not seem to get spent on the statue's upkeep.

Finally Major Taylor could contain himself no longer. He made a statement saying, "Inside and out, the Statue of Liberty is a distinct disgrace to our country." He loudly condemned both the Lighthouse Board and the Citizens Committee and said that neither one of them had expended money or work on the statue. As long as Liberty was managed jointly, he felt that "this grand work of Art will go steadily down hill."

The publicity Major Taylor's remarks received prompted the federal government to think about making some changes. The statue "has no value as a light to the Lighthouse Establishment," said Secretary of the Treasury Gage, who was in charge of the Lighthouse Board. He said that taking care of the statue was a financial burden to his department, and he agreed to help urge the President to turn her over to the War Department. Nothing was heard from the Citizens Committee.

It was not surprising, therefore, that without further ado President Theodore Roosevelt signed an order on December 30, 1901, giving the War Department full responsibility for taking care of the statue. Since it was no longer to serve as a lighthouse, the Secretary of the Treasury issued an order for the removal of the electric plant on the island. On March 1, 1902, Liberty's torch was dark. It was rumored that since Liberty did not receive many visitors, the tourist business might be shut down altogether.

While New Yorkers up to this point had not shown much interest in Liberty, they now rallied to support her. They missed looking out in the harbor and seeing her lighted torch at night. They felt they were entitled to visit her if they wanted to. New York newspapers ran articles demanding that Liberty be kept open and her torch remain lighted. The federal government finally responded, and the electric plant remained. The Secretary of War justified the new order by saying the torch would serve as part of the lighting of the military post. On the night of April 23, the *New York Tribune* ran as their headline: LIBERTY'S TORCH AGAIN SHINES. Ferries also continued taking visitors to the statue.

At the same time, changes were also taking place on Ellis Island. When Theodore Roosevelt became president in 1901, sweeping reforms were made in immigration procedures. The corrupt officials were removed, and Ellis Island became at last a hospitable service center for new Americans. A reliable company, American Express, eventually took over the money exchange, the food was improved, and an enormous staff of social-service workers speaking every language in the world gave helpful advice and even money to the immigrants if it was needed.

In 1903 a bronze tablet engraved with the words of Emma Lazarus's moving poem, "The New Colossus," was placed inside the walls of Liberty's pedestal. It is sad, however, that during the years when the greatest number of immigrants were arriving in New York harbor, her stirring words were not there to give hope to the new arrivals.

The following year, Liberty's creator, Auguste Bartholdi, died— on October 4, 1904. He lived long enough to see his work of colossal art erected in New York harbor but not long enough to observe how important his statue would become to the American people or to see his dream of a landscaped setting take shape.

While conditions were greatly improved on Ellis Island, the lady on nearby Bedloe's Island continued to have her problems. Although it was helpful having only one agency—the War Department—in charge, it was still not clear as to who should foot the bill for the statue's maintenance and just how much should be spent for her upkeep.

In the early years of the twentieth century, there were a number of requests for the repair and improvement of the statue. One of the greatest concerns was that Liberty was turning green. The *New York Evening Post* demanded a thorough cleaning to remove the "unsightly green crust." The Citizens Committee replied that, on the contrary, they did not believe the greenness was injuring the surface of the metal and they did not feel an expensive cleaning was necessary.

It was a wise decision. As the years passed, exposure to the elements had indeed caused the copper shell to turn a light green color. The green layer, called patina, is often seen on outdoor copper and bronze statues. When the copper combines in a chemical process with substances in the air, a copper sulphate, or patina, is formed that scientists now know serves as an important protective barrier against further corrosion. If the

One of the first aerial photographs of the statue taken in 1912.

patina were to be removed, the thin skin remaining would be exposed to corrosion it could not withstand.

There were also a number of demands to improve the lighting of the statue. Enough money was never provided for that purpose, but in 1907 the federal government did supply $62,800, which was enough to make some much needed repairs and to install stairways in the statue and an electric elevator in the pedestal.

It was not until almost another decade had passed, however, that an historical event took place that served to rekindle interest in the Statue of Liberty as a national symbol. With the threat of a world war hanging over the nation, concepts such as freedom and democracy became very important to the people of the United States. Just as the French people wanted to remind the world of the importance of liberty during their difficult years of revolution, the Americans now desperately wanted to rekindle their belief in the importance of their democratic form of government. Liberty was a symbol of that belief, and by the onset of World War I she became a symbol of America herself.

As this renewed awareness of Liberty surfaced, her old champion, *The World*, once again decided to launch an appeal to the people for repair funds. The newspaper's goal in 1916 was to raise $30,000 to install a new lighting plant, with the federal government being responsible for yearly maintenance. President Wilson agreed to this arrangement.

Other agencies then promised to join in the fund-raising campaign. The Navy Department undertook a dramatic demonstration to show the effect of the new proposed floodlighting. The powerful searchlights of the battleship *Michigan* bathed the statue in brilliant light for thirty-five minutes.

Just before the campaign really got under way, however, a catastrophe took place that centered even more attention on the Statue of Liberty. Early on Sunday morning, July 30, 1916, German sabateurs blew up a munitions plant and loaded ships located at the Black Tom Wharf on the New Jersey shore. The plant was located just half a mile from Bedloe's Island. For more than eight hours the island was bombarded by shells and shrapnel from blazing ships filled with ammunition for shipment abroad.

The disaster caused two deaths and an estimated $40,000,000 in property damage. Nearly a hundred people, mostly members of the Army Signal Corps Company and their families, were living on Bedloe's Island at the time. The women and children were taken to Governor's Island.

The incident could have meant the end for the Statue of Liberty, which stood perilously high in the air, but miraculously army engineers later surveying the damage found the island and the statue had fared quite well during the disaster. The pedestal and exterior had been nicked slightly by the shrapnel, but the power plant was not harmed, and the torchlight continued to burn during the bombardment.

The only casualty was the ripping off of about one hundred iron bolts in the inner shell, mostly in the upraised arm. Their loss weakened the already most fragile part of the statue, and from then on the ladder leading through the arm to the torch was closed to the public.

About $100,000 worth of damage was done to the island's structures, but only one building, a corrugated iron warehouse, had been destroyed.

News of the Black Tom explosion caused a surge in contributions to *The World*'s fund. Donations soon began to pour in from every state and from several foreign countries, too. School children once again gave their pennies. In less than six months the goal of $30,000 was achieved through the contributions of more than 50,000 people.

Underwater cables were put down on the harbor bottom between New Jersey and Bedloe's Island to provide electricity for 246 new floodlights whose purpose was to bathe the whole statue in radiant light. The floodlights were placed on the star points of the old fort and on the balcony of the pedestal.

The major lighting renovation resulted in a complete change being made in the torch. The task was given to a sculptor named Gutzon Borglum, who was later to become well known for his huge sculpture of four presidential faces carved high on the face of Mt. Rushmore in the Black Hills of North Dakota.

In order to make the torch look like a real flame, Borglum had holes cut all over the torch and installed about one hundred small sections of amber cathedral glass. A powerful light was placed in the torch to shine through the glass plates. Each pane was carefully glazed into its metal framework so that it would be waterproof and be able to withstand strong harbor winds.

The lights were dedicated on December 2, 1916. President Wilson presided over the procedings from the presidential yacht, the *Mayflower*, while a division of the Atlantic Fleet was present in the harbor.

When the sun dropped beneath the horizon, the President gave a radio wireless signal that turned on the lights as whistles blew, ships fired cannons, and a popular female pilot, Ruth Law, flew over the statue in a lighted plane.

After the ceremony a parade took place, which started at the Battery and ended at the Waldorf Hotel, where a dinner was held. President Wilson spoke in his usual idealistic and inspiring way when he said the Statue of Liberty was "a proper symbol of our life." The illumination, he said, "did not proceed from Liberty, but . . . from the light we were throwing upon Liberty." In words that recalled the feelings of Édouard de Laboulaye,

A World War I poster urging citizens to support their country by purchasing a Liberty Bond

President Wilson soberly remarked, "There has come more and more into my heart the conviction that peace is going to come to the world only with liberty."

A few months later the United States was engaged in World War I—the war that was thought to end all wars. During those years, spurred on by *The World*'s campaign and the President's moving words at the lighting dedication, the Statue of Liberty continued to grow in importance in the eyes of the American people and to take on a new role. Restrictions were put on the number of people who were allowed into the country, and the flood of immigrants almost came to a halt. Therefore, instead of welcoming newcomers to our shores, Liberty was seen as waving good-bye to thousands of young men as they sailed away to war. To these soldiers, Liberty presented one last strong, motherly image of America.

For quite some time the female figure of Columbia had represented the United States. The war changed that. Liberty took over as the nation's unofficial national symbol. In order to raise money to help pay for what was then the most costly war in the history of the world, four "Liberty loan drives" were held during 1917 and 1918. Millions of posters asking Americans to buy war bonds appeared all over the country in which Liberty was shown in all kinds of poses. In some she lowered her right hand and pointed a finger at her public demanding, "You buy a Liberty Bond lest I perish." Sometimes she was dressed in an American flag and carried a shield rather than a book. Other posters featured the statue and newly arriving immigrants. The bond drives were a huge success and paid for half the war.

Before going overseas, the 77th Division of the United States Army, stationed at Camp Upton, New York, chose the statue for its insignia. During the war the men of this division fought bravely in France and became known as the men of the Liberty Division.

When "the war to end all wars" was finally over, the Statue of Liberty became the symbol of home to the returning soldiers. This time, instead of the immigrants, it was young Americans whose eyes filled with tears as they sailed past Liberty.

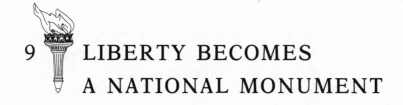

9 LIBERTY BECOMES A NATIONAL MONUMENT

Liberty's popularity continued after the war was over. A total of 170,000 people visited Bedloe's Island in 1922. The United States government, however, did very little in regard to her care. The country was busy getting back to normal, and it was thought that the 1916 lighting system was all the improvement Liberty needed for a while.

Behind the scenes, however, there had been several years of quiet campaigning to turn the Statue of Liberty into a National Monument. Several old New England forts had recently been given that designation. The campaign for Liberty finally achieved its goal when, on October 15, 1924, President Coolidge proclaimed the Statute of Liberty an official National Monument. It was the only one to stand for an idea; all the others served as reminders of events in America's history.

As soon as she achieved this status, there were the usual "Well, what do we do with her now?" questions. At first not very much changed. The War Department continued to be in charge of the statue. The army's primary responsibility, however, was to run the Signal Corps radio station located on the island.

Luckily one fact did soon become apparent. The army's policy of frequently replacing post commanders at Fort Wood meant that nobody was responsible for the complicated care of Liberty for very long. A War Department committee was appointed to study this problem, and a year after the statue became a

National Monument, a civilian superintendent, under the supervision of the Fort Wood commander, was appointed for an indefinite term to live on Bedloe's Island and do nothing but care for Liberty. Finally, there was one person whose sole job was to take care of the Statue of Liberty.

On November 16, 1925, William A. Simpson, assisted by three civilians, became the first superintendent of the Statue of Liberty National Monument. He had many unexpected problems to solve, most resulting from the statue's new popularity. The Liberty bond drive during World War I had been one of the most successful advertising campaigns of all time. Now that Liberty had become a highly regarded figure, many groups, companies, and organizations wanted to use her as a symbol for their advertising purposes.

This kind of attempt was not entirely new. As far back as 1884, during the pedestal fund campaign, an offer had been made to donate $25,000 if ". . . for the period of one year you permit us to place across the top of the pedestal the word 'CASTORIA'. Thus art and science, the symbol of liberty to man, and of health to his children, would be more closely enshrined in the hearts of our people." The donation was, of course, refused.

Some time later Superintendent Simpson had to deal with quite a different problem when three members of the War Veterans Light Wines and Beer League came to Bedloe's Island. The three men climbed to the crown, where they draped two 60-foot black crepe streamers from the windows to protest their "loss of liberty and free speech" when they had not been allowed to speak during at a Senate committee hearing on prohibition. Simpson and two guards raced up the stairs and pulled down the crepe almost immediately, but not before a press agent standing on a nearby hired tug got the publicity pictures he wanted. As a result of this incident, fifty men were added to the

---

Bedloe's Island about 1920 with United States Army buildings clustered around the Statue of Liberty

military police detachment on the island in order to tighten
security.

Another reason for adding the guard force was to prevent
suicide attempts. In 1926 a fast-moving guard was able to stop
the attempted suicide of a young Russian refugee about to be
deported. But three years later a young man from the Bronx
succeeded in taking his life by jumping to his death after climbing out one of the windows in the crown.

Yet another problem facing the new superintendent was the
maintenance and repair of Liberty. The statue, especially the
pedestal, had become encrusted with soot and grime carried to
Bedloe's Island on westerly winds from industrial New Jersey.
The army studied several plans for cleaning the structure, and
various methods were discussed in the press, but the talk ended
when a group of people tried to powder the statue's nose. Superintendent Simpson decided bathing Liberty was a headache
he could do without. There were more important matters that
needed his attention.

His main concern was what to do about the lighting system.
Half of the floodlight projectors installed in 1916 had defective
reflectors, and corrosion had caused many of them to lose their
mountings. An even more serious problem was spotted by soldiers stationed on nearby Governor's Island. They noticed that
when darkness fell and the batteries of floodlights were turned
on, distorting shadows formed in the wrong spots. Bags appeared under Liberty's eyes, and a bad shadow under her chin
made her appear to have acquired a double chin. Under the
four-and-a-half-foot nose an ugly blur was cast on either side
of the face giving the cheeks a hollow appearance.

In 1931 funds were provided by the federal government to
make the needed improvements. A modern floodlighting system, designed to put an end to all shadows and costing about

---

Two big holes were cut underneath the torch platform in 1931 in order
to install projectors that would throw light on the face to eliminate unsightly shadows.

$30,000, was installed by the Westinghouse Electric and Manufacturing Company. To further enhance Liberty, lights were installed for the first time in the twenty-one windows of the crown. They were wired to a blinker system to create the impression of glittering jewels.

Two big holes were cut underneath the torch platform in order to install projectors to get rid of the shadows on Liberty's face. "Improvements" of this kind would later be frowned upon because any holes cut in Liberty's skin contributed to the terrible corrosion eventually discovered inside the statue. Marring historic statues in the manner done in 1931 is no longer allowed.

On October 26, 1931, two days before the statue's forty-fifth anniversary, the new lighting system was dedicated in a complicated ceremony. French Premier Laval's daughter, Jose Laval, standing on the top floor of the Empire State Building, sent a radio signal to an airplane flying near the statue. The plane, picking up the radio signal, activated an electric eye that turned on the 500,000 candlepower system, enough power to light 250 average homes. Liberty burst into light and was twice as bright as she had been previously.

Urged on by Superintendent Simpson, the War Department made other needed repairs during the early 1930s. The pedestal stairs received new safety treads and handrails. The outside of the granite pedestal was repointed. Small openings in the copper shell were welded. New windows were installed in the crown. A new Otis elevator replaced the old one, which had been in operation for twenty-five years.

Finally, with the new floodlights making the grime even more obvious, the statue and pedestal were steam-cleaned. Moving toward her fiftieth birthday, it seemed as if Liberty was in pretty good shape.

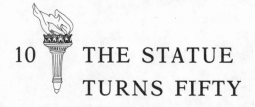

10 THE STATUE
TURNS FIFTY

While Liberty was in better shape, the rest of the nation was not faring as well. In 1929 there had been a stock market crash that had plunged the United States, and most of the world, into something close to economic ruin. As the country entered the 1930s, a record high 25 percent of the people were without jobs, wages had dropped drastically, and farmers were paid next to nothing for their crops. Everywhere people were hungry. This period became known as the Great Depression.

Herbert Hoover was the president of the United States at the time, and on his final day in office, on March 4, 1933, he was told that the banking system of the United States had collapsed. When he received this news, the tired and defeated president said, "We are at the end of our string. There is nothing more we can do."

His successor, Franklin D. Roosevelt, did not agree. In his first hundred days of office he began a staggering number of programs designed to create new jobs and feed hungry people. President Roosevelt called his new legislation the "New Deal."

Because he believed that whenever possible a jobless man should be re-employed in his own line of work, President Roosevelt set up a program called the Works Progress Administration. In it federal money was provided for a wide variety of public projects, and thousands of unemployed people were given jobs paying up to $94.90 a month.

During the Great Depression some people in New York City were forced to live in shantytowns such as the one shown here in Berenice Abbott's photograph from the Federal Art Project "Changing New York."

Another thing President Roosevelt did in his first year of office was to move many of the national monuments and parks, including several forts and the Statue of Liberty, from the jurisdiction of the War Department to the Department of the Interior. The supervision of these monuments was given to a single agency called the Office of National Parks, Buildings, and Reservations. The following year the name of this agency was shortened to the National Park Service.

The newspapers speculated that the change was made to save money. They did not think the Department of the Interior would have as much money to spend on Liberty as the United States Army. This did not prove to be the case. A few months later

$25,000 of public works funds were allocated for routine repairs, which centered mostly on improving the visitor area within the pedestal.

Once again, however, a change in administration brought confusion to Bedloe's Island. The National Monument property included only the Statue of Liberty herself. The rest of the twelve-acre island was an army reservation. When the National Park Service arrived on the scene, they immediately began making plans to turn the whole island into a national park, much as

The military is still very much in evidence on Bedloe's Island as the nation celebrates its birthday on July 4, 1934. In honor of the day, the Stars and Stripes was flown from Liberty's torch.

Auguste Bartholdi had envisioned. The United States Army agreed to move out as long as housing could be provided for them elsewhere. Plans began to be made to have public works money spent on building army housing someplace else and on tearing down the old army barracks and beautifying the island. Superintendent Simpson was delighted.

A year later, however, the War Department changed its mind. It reminded the Department of the Interior that the deed signed in 1800 had given Bedloe's Island to the United States specifically for military purposes. The War Department felt that giving the island to the National Park Service violated the 1800 deed. If not used for military purposes, the Secretary of War said the federal government would lose jurisdiction of the island. It was a legal technicality, but it worked, and the army stayed on in their ramshackle accommodations. Superintendent Simpson was naturally a very disappointed man.

In the meantime, Liberty's fiftieth birthday was approaching. While plans were being drawn up to celebrate the occasion, Superintendent Simpson retired. George A. Palmer, a Park Service career man, took his place. He immediately took over the planning for October 28, 1936, and invited President Franklin D. Roosevelt and the French Ambassador to take part in the ceremonies.

Superintendent Palmer had the foresight to realize that because Bedloe's Island is so small and isolated, only a few people could attend a celebration there. He also knew that Liberty was more than just a statue in New York harbor; she was a symbol of freedom and liberty that belonged to the entire country. The best way to celebrate her birthday, he felt, would be to hold a year-long national celebration ending with a rededication ceremony on October 28 at the statue.

His plans were readily accepted. In schools throughout the nation, the statue and its background and meaning in American history were studied. Many civic, educational, and patriotic organizations held various activities, such as essay, speech, and poetry contests. There was nationwide radio, newspaper, and magazine publicity. Frenchmen living in America joined in the celebration, and their interest in the event was carried back to their homeland. The French holiday, Bastille Day, was celebrated at the statue. Unfortunately, in 1935 Superintendent Palmer was moved to another assignment and was therefore not in charge when the official celebration he had worked so hard to bring about took place. Instead, Oswald E. Camp, who became the third superintendent of the Statue of Liberty National Monument on December 16, 1935, presided over the event.

On October 28, 1936, on a beautiful fall day, the nation's troubles were set aside for a short time as President Roosevelt and French Ambassador de Laboulaye, the grandson of Édouard de Laboulaye, along with about 3,500 other people, journeyed to Bedloe's Island for the celebration. People all over the country listened on their radios and heard the president say:

> It was the hope of those who gave us this statue and the hope of the American people receiving it, that the Goddess of Liberty and the Goddess of Peace were the same. It is fitting, therefore, that this should be a service of rededication to the liberty and the peace which this statue symbolizes. Liberty and peace are living things. In each generation—if they are to be maintained—they must be guarded and vitalized anew.

The fiftieth anniversary activities served to make Liberty even more popular. Feeling the new prestige of the statue might make a difference, the Department of the Interior once again approached the War Department and suggested the army should leave Bedloe's Island—gradually if necessary. Progress finally began to occur when $175,000 was made available from public works to pay for relocating the troops.

On May 4, 1937, the War Department told the Department of Interior that Bedloe's Island was all theirs, and they would evacuate the island by June 30, except for the Second Corps area radio station. The Department of the Interior immediately drew up a draft proclamation to enlarge the Statue of Liberty National Monument and to give the army permission to retain

the facilities for operating their radio station. It took time for the necessary paperwork to be completed, but finally on September 7, 1937, President Roosevelt issued a proclamation adding the Fort Wood reservation to the Statue of Liberty National Monument. He said the enlargement was necessary for "the proper care, management, and protection of the colossal statue of 'Liberty Enlightening the World.' " After the proclamation things moved quickly. By September 30 all military equipment and personnel except for the radio station were gone, and the island was turned over to the National Park Service.

The National Park Service at once got to work on a master plan. An architect and a landscaper were hired to work out a scheme for the whole island. A Works Progress Administration project was approved to study and repair the statue and pedestal. Serious water seepage was discovered in several places.

A close look at the armature showed that after fifty years some of the ribs in the upraised arm and the tablet were so badly rusted that they would have to be rebuilt or in some cases replaced altogether. This was a time-consuming process. The corroded segments were brought down a few at a time to an on-site workshop. There they were used as patterns to forge new pieces. After all the iron bars were shaped, holes were drilled for bolts. The pieces were then painted to protect them from moisture. Those segments that were not a total loss were strengthened by welding and then returned to their original places.

It was also discovered that the spikes on Liberty's crown had suffered weather damage. Over the summer of 1938 all of the spikes were removed from the crown, and Liberty had to get along without her rays for about a month while the rusted supports were replaced. Lastly, a new stairway was built going up to the foot of the statue.

President Roosevelt helps celebrate the Statue of Liberty's fiftieth birthday on October 28, 1936.

New ribs are made to replace some rusty old ones in a blacksmith shed erected at the base of the statue.

Workmen remove a spike from Liberty's crown during 1938 repairs.

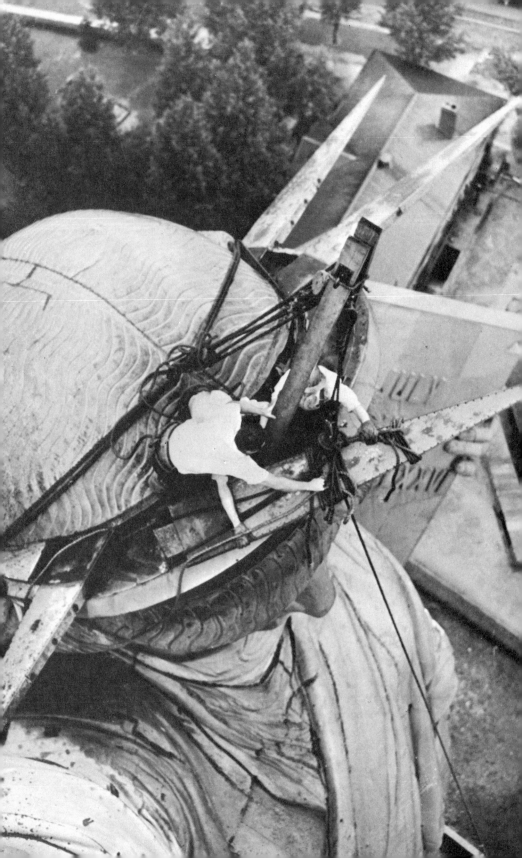

During most of the repairs the statue was closed to the public. Work began in May 1937, and Liberty was not reopened to visitors until December 15, 1938. The repairs and alterations to the statue cost $158,328, and it was the most extensive program ever to take place on the statue. Without the WPA funding the work could never have been done. Many other monuments and national parks also benefited from WPA and Public Works Administration (PWA) projects during this period in the country's history.

As work on the statue neared completion, work on the rest of the island was begun. The first order of business was to tear down the twenty army buildings and structures on the island, the ones clustered around the statue being the first to go.

As part of the master plan, a statement of general objectives had been written. The following lines clearly stated what the National Park Service had in mind for Bedloe's Island:

> . . . the cramped squalor of the present surroundings must be replaced by a setting of appropriately well-ordered dignity. It is clear that ample simplicity, rather than ostentation, will be an essential quality of such an environment. But it is equally clear that a niggardly policy of development would be unwarranted and disastrous.

This philosophy was adhered to during the changes that took much longer than anyone anticipated. With the army buildings gone, the plan was to erect new administration, utility, museum, and residence buildings at the northwest end of the island in a landscaped area removed from the statue. In order to accomplish this, the island would have to be enlarged with landfill and a new seawall erected.

The National Park Service also wanted to abandon and demolish the east dock immediately in front of the statue and use instead the army's west dock in an improved or new version. This change was intended to give visitors a longer and broader view of the statue from the water since boats would have to round the island before docking.

It was estimated that it would take slightly more than $1,500,000 to make the improvements to the island. The National Park Service went to the PWA to request that the funds be given to them over a six-year period.

During 1937 and 1938 more than a third of this amount was provided by WPA and PWA funds. A new seawall was begun, a deep hole was dug for a new flagpole foundation, and some regrading and grass seeding was done on the eastern end of the island.

Money was also spent to alter the buildings on nearby Ellis Island. Since the immigration center was no longer a busy place, part of the island was turned over to the Coast Guard, who occupied it between 1939 and 1946. They made many changes in the buildings including putting up walls and discarding furniture and artifacts from the immigration era.

On Bedloe's Island Superintendent Camp was delighted with how much was being accomplished, but the demolition and construction work created a serious problem for the island staff. There was often an enormous amount of cleaning up to do after the workers left for the day. Superintendent Camp had only two laborers to tidy up the whole island and maintain the utilities, whereas the job had previously been done by a large military police detail. Finally, in December 1937, Superintendent Palmer was reassigned to the statue and managed to get the maintenance staff increased to five men. With a larger crew the superintendent was better able to cope with the work.

Another major headache was ferry service to the island. The company to which the army had given the ferry contract continued to serve the island when the National Park Service arrived. It was required to provide safe and regular transportation at reasonable prices to visitors, as well as provide boat service after visiting hours for the guard staff. There were boat breakdowns, however, and eventually the National Park Service awarded the contract to another company, who operated the ferry concession for the next ten years.

Being on an island caused other problems. Although Bedloe's

Island is only a little more than a mile from one of the largest and most advanced cities in the world, life there was often a challenge and required some of the skills of early pioneers. Water, electricity, and telephone communication came to the island through underwater cables from New Jersey. Frequently these cables were damaged by ships' anchors or dredging operations. It was more difficult for the National Park Service to get repairs made than it had been for the United States Army. Even when repairmen were recruited, it always took a long time to find the source of problems. The people who worked and lived on Bedloe's Island often had to get along without water fit to drink, without telephone service, and without electricity that provided both heat and light. Living and working on the island required a spirit of adventure.

By the end of the thirties, however, the nation was getting back on its feet, Liberty had been repaired, and the island was in the process of being cleared for landscaping. But there was no time to sit back and enjoy the improvements in the statue and the fragile prosperity that had developed following the 1929 financial crash. As the decade ended, events even more terrible than the Great Depression began to change the course of history.

In 1939 German tanks rolled into Poland. England and France declared war on Germany. Work on national monuments and national parks slowed down as the United States braced itself for a possible new world war.

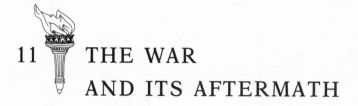

11 THE WAR
AND ITS AFTERMATH

As the nation entered the forties, many people living in the United States felt the wars being waged in Europe and Asia were none of their business. Some Americans took pride in being isolationists and felt the two huge oceans separating the country from Europe and Asia would keep the nation safe. This change in attitude carried over to the way some people now regarded the Statue of Liberty. At first she was a French-American lady, a symbol of ties between two countries. Now she became strictly an American symbol.

Many people did not approve when President Roosevelt at the start of 1940 asked Congress for $1.8 billion to finance the greatest peacetime military build-up in the entire history of the United States. They called him a warmonger.

The isolationists became less sure of their views as Hitler's troops overran country after country. By the end of 1940 the Germans controlled all of Western Europe. Britain and the ocean stood between Germany and the United States, but the Atlantic Ocean looked smaller every day as Hitler's submarines began to dominate the sea.

Soon after he was elected to an unprecedented third term, President Roosevelt introduced a Lend-Lease plan that seemed indirectly to put the United States into the war when it became a law on March 11, 1941. It allowed the President to give aid to any country whose defense the president deemed vital to the defense of the United States. So while the United States was not actually sending her young men to war, she was committed to all other kinds of help. The day after the law was passed, Congress appropriated $7 billion to the Lend-Lease plan.

The contributions of the United States grew rapidly. At the beginning, President Roosevelt had sixteen tanks to send to the war effort. By the end of the year 951 tanks had been sent. By Christmas food shipments had reached one million tons.

On the morning of December 7, 1941, all hopes for peace went up in smoke when Pearl Harbor was bombed. The only thing that was possible at that point was to join America's allies and fight.

What did this mean to Liberty and her torch? First of all, the development of the island came to a rapid and total halt. Lighting improvements planned by the Westinghouse Electric and Manufacturing Company, which were supposed to be installed on January 1, 1942, had to be postponed. Except for a small aerial obstruction light in the torch, the statue was blacked out for the entire war. In addition, a Coast Guard observation station was installed on the third landing of the pedestal.

The island, however, remained open to visitors every day. Liberty had by this time become the most visited National Monument in the whole country. In 1940, 395,000 people visited the statue. The number declined during the war, however, mostly because of travel restrictions and fuel rationing, and those who did come were not permitted to bring cameras because of the large number of warships in the harbor. There was also a ban on school children traveling to museums and other sites of interest in New York City. But throughout the war, the number of service men and women visiting Liberty increased.

During the war the Bedloe's Island staff found living and working on the island a greater challenge than ever. First of all, many of them were drafted into the armed services, and the staff was reduced for economy reasons, too. Those who remained received emergency air-raid, fire-fighting, and first-aid training.

Even making a telephone call was difficult. During the war

War planes on their way to Europe fly over the Statue of Liberty during World War II as shown in a lithograph by James Allen.

long-distance telephone calls were severely limited. Since Bedloe's Island was connected to the New Jersey telephone system, a call to Manhattan was a long-distance call. Superintendent Palmer had to spend at least one day a week in Manhattan to conduct his New York City business.

In spite of all these problems, the Statue of Liberty, as she had during World War I, became a symbol of the democractic values and institutions our soldiers were defending. *Life* magazine put it this way:

> Never before has the Statue of Liberty seemed so important. Never before have so many millions dreamed of her overseas or so many Americans . . . traveled to Bedloe's Island somehow to absorb her perishable significance from the folds of her imperishable bronze . . .

An example of how much the statue can mean to an individual came from a story told by one of the statue's guides. The incident took place during the war years on a cold, nasty day in the middle of winter. The guide recalls that the first ferry of the day brought only one young woman as a visitor to the statue. She stayed outside leaning against the pedestal. She didn't look well, and the guide asked her if she felt all right. She answered, "Yes, yes, of course," but the guide wasn't convinced and stayed with her. They talked about the bad weather that morning, and the young woman seemed worried about it. It turned out that her husband, a science technician, had just taken off for England where V-1 bombing was at its peak. She was sure the weather over the Atlantic had been terrible, and she had been up all night worrying. It was obvious to the guide that the woman had done a lot of crying, too.

"I've been waiting since early morning for the ferry to bring me here," she said. "I just wanted to remind myself why he had to go."

Thousands of New Yorkers lined the Battery promenade on the evening of June 6, 1944, as the statue was relighted for fifteen minutes to flash the "V for Victory" sign following the Normandy invasion.

The following month a war-bond rally led by Mayor La-Guardia was held on the island. That same year a fifty-five-foot model of Liberty was put up in Times Square to serve as a center of attraction for war-bond rallies. The light in it was turned on by President Roosevelt on November 17, 1944, by remote control from Washington. Everyone who purchased a bond at the model was given a free ticket to visit the real Statue of Liberty.

As the long and terrible war drew to a close, Westinghouse engineers revived their plans to improve the lighting of the statue. A battery of sixteen mercury-vapor lamps was added to the floodlighting system. Westinghouse predicted the radiance of the floodlights would be doubled. Their combined beams were said to be 2,500 times as bright as light received from the moon.

Westinghouse also experimented with new, brighter lights for the torch, where a system of mixed incandescent and green mercury-vapor lamps were installed. They gave the torch a greenish sheen and created a flame effect. They were also much brighter than any previous torchlights. It was said the new torchlight could be seen from ten to twenty miles at sea.

It was a time for rejoicing when on V-E day, May 7, 1945, the lights were turned on again at the Statue of Liberty after several years of darkness. But it was an even happier time when soldiers on troop ships returning from the war shouted for joy as they spotted Liberty waiting to greet them. As the troop ships came back, arrangements were made to have the statue illuminated all night long so that she could be seen no matter what time the soldiers arrived.

In the years following World War II, more visitors came out to Bedloe's Island than ever before in the statue's history. As the ferries passed Ellis Island, visitors stared with great interest at the buildings on the island. During both World War I and World War II, people accused of threatening the nation's security had been detained on Ellis Island. After World War II, shell-shocked victims were housed in the island's hospital facilities. Also, during a scare that swept the nation after the war, suspected Communists were held there. In addition, the island continued to serve as an immigration center. It was no wonder, therefore, that Ellis Island and its assorted occupants aroused the curiosity of those on their way to visit Liberty.

The ever-increasing popularity of the Statue of Liberty was also causing new problems for Superintendent Charles S. Marshall, who had replaced George Palmer on September 23, 1945. Bedloe's Island simply did not have the equipment or the staff to handle the large number of visitors coming over on the ferries every day. Work on the master plan to do over the island had really just begun when it had to be halted by the war. When visitors came to the island, they still had to land at the old east pier in front of the statue. It was dilapidated and even dangerous. The western end of the island, where the new buildings were being erected, was closed to the public. It was still covered in places with rubble left over from the demolition work done by the WPA workers. Therefore, the thousands of visitors arriv-

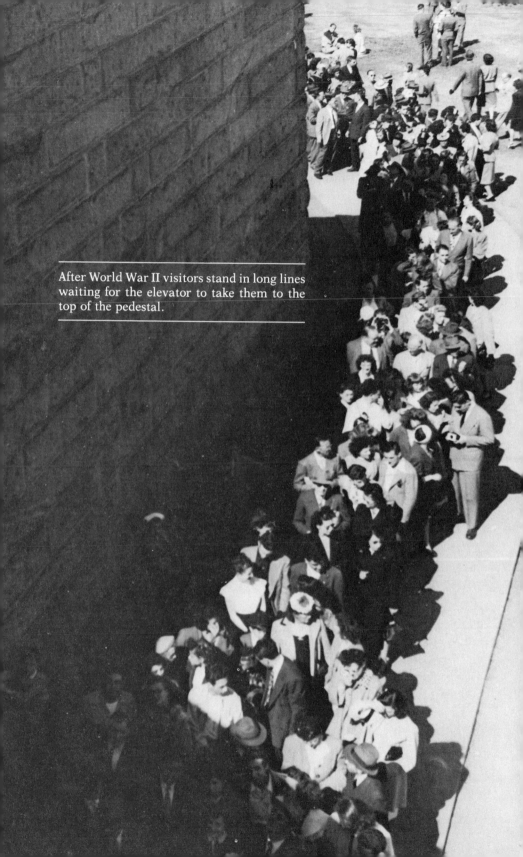

After World War II visitors stand in long lines waiting for the elevator to take them to the top of the pedestal.

ing each day had to crowd into the small area in and around the monument. The staff, who wanted to show the visitors around and talk about the statue's history, instead had to devote most of its time to picking up litter, trying to keep the crowds from walking on the grassy areas, and preventing vandalism.

The situation received quite a lot of criticism in newspapers during the summer of 1946. The *New York World Telegram*, the successor to *The World*, voiced a protest:

> . . . the unkempt condition of this revered monument borders on a national disgrace.
>
> From the dilapidated, sea-worn east dock . . . the grassless terrace, littered with partly eaten fruit, sandwiches, and soda glasses, Miss Liberty's environs reflect Washington's apathy toward a once-beautiful shrine . . .

This photograph, looking toward the back of Liberty, shows the rubble left behind by the WPA workers on the western end of Bedloe's Island. A massive clean-up was needed.

The thing that received the most criticism from the press, however, was the amount of graffiti inside the statue. Throughout history man has left his mark in the form of writing on historic monuments, but in the United States scribbling in public places has become a particularly bad habit. During the war years the graffiti artists used lipstick because magic markers and spray cans were not yet available for sale widely in stores. As people climbed the stairs to Liberty's crown, it was fairly easy to reach out and leave a lipstick message or name on the inside of Liberty's skin and on her armature. More athletic artists actually left the stairs and clambered across beams and braces to leave their marks on the statue's interior. The maintenance staff tried patch painting over the lipstick, but they could not keep up with the amount of lipstick that was applied every day.

The general public was outraged at the defacing of their beloved statue. A radio personality of the time, Arthur Godfrey, often spoke of the problem on his popular morning show. He suggested that the offenders be punished by having their noses rubbed in their lipstick artistry.

Because there were so many complaints, Congress allocated $50,000 in 1947 to clean both the statue and the island. Under the supervision of Superintendent Marshall, the east dock was repaired and the old floor replaced. The stairs and interior walls were steam-cleaned and a special lipstick-proof enamel applied. Unlike ordinary paint, lipstick could not penetrate it, and the markings could easily be cleaned off its tough surface. In addition, woven wire guards were placed around the stairways so that visitors could not crawl out onto supporting beams or reach the walls. The new measures were effective in putting an end to the lipstick problem. The unfortunate result of adding the thick wire mesh, however, was that visitors were almost com-

---

Wire mesh was installed around the statue stairway in 1947 to prevent graffiti artists from drawing on the interior skin and framework.

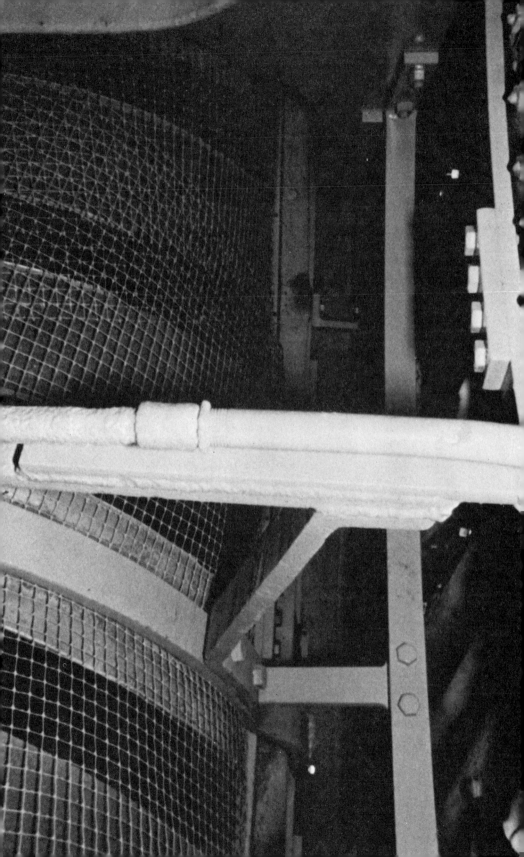

pletely cut off from viewing Eiffel's interior framework, which many architectural experts felt was the most interesting feature of the Statue of Liberty.

While these changes were being made, the island was closed to visitors off and on for three months during the first part of 1947. Everyone felt the $50,000 was well spent, but Congress was now urged to come up with more money so that the master plan could be completed. It was also felt that additional money should be appropriated for maintenance of the area.

Another feature of Liberty that received considerable attention during the postwar years was the plaque containing the poem written by Emma Lazarus about the plight of exiles. It began to draw silent, thoughtful crowds of tourists around it since many visitors had relatives and friends in Europe who had been driven from their homes by the war.

Ever since the beginning of World War I, strict laws limited how many people the United States would accept from a particular country. At the end of World War II, however, President Truman asked Congress to make it easier for people who had lost their homes to come to the United States. On June 25, 1948, Congress passed legislation that made it possible for 205,000 homeless Europeans to come to the United States. That number included 3,000 orphans and such famous newcomers as Albert Einstein and Enrico Fermi.

Like any good mother, when it was necessary, Liberty adapted easily to a role she had formerly played. From being a symbol of democracy or a symbol representing the United States during time of war, Liberty once again assumed her role as Mother of Exiles.

12 THE MASTER PLAN
IS COMPLETED

In the closing years of the 1940s much pressure was put upon Congress, particularly by women's organizations, to allocate the necessary funds to complete the master plan, and finally $500,000 was set aside for that purpose.

During the early 1950s much work was done. The major project was dredging a new channel and turning basin for the ferries and building a new west pier. Also, to the great relief of the island staff, work was finally begun on the far western end of the island where employees lived. The area was enlarged by fill from the dredging operations, a new seawall was built to keep it from washing away, and a new water main was laid from Jersey City.

During all this construction, there were frequent breaks in water, power, and telephone lines caused by the dredging operations. Then a violent storm in November 1950 threatened the whole project. It washed away some of the new fill, flooded part of the island, left it without lights or heat, and caused the collapse of the old east pier. After the storm, the statue had to be closed for two weeks while repairs were made.

Work on the western end then resumed. The staff area was separated from the rest of the island by buildings, a fence, and landscaping, giving those who were to live on the island much needed privacy. Red-brick employees' quarters were built in the area, and the superintendent and his family and a handful of other key staff members moved into their new homes in October 1952. Residence walks were laid down, and a playground was constructed behind the houses.

More improvements were also made to the statue herself. A heating plant was installed in the pedestal to cut down on condensation. New aluminum treads were put on the spiral stairs. The elevator was repaired and the torch rewired. Lastly, lipstick marks were sandblasted from the outside granite steps.

Because there was so much renewed interest in Liberty as the Mother of Exiles, a proposal was made to the National Park Service in 1952 that a museum of immigration be constructed within the structure beneath the statue. It was thought that once again the public could be asked to donate the necessary funds and a private organization such as *The World* could take charge of the fund-raising campaign. The purpose of the museum would be to show how people who came from countries all over the world were able to work together to create a growing and successful nation. Though everyone thought the museum proposal a good idea, nothing was immediately done about it because at the moment there was a more pressing problem to attend to.

For years the island had been plagued with ferry problems. In recent years the price of tickets had risen seveal times, and the workers often threatened to strike for higher wages. Finally, in June 1953, at the beginning of the busy summer season, the ferry workers carried out their threat. A month later the fed-up National Park Service signed a contract with yet another boat company, which went into effect on October 1, 1953. Eventually, two large ferries operated to the island every day, the newer of the boats carrying 750 people. At long last, the boat problem appeared to be solved.

During the 1950s great strides were also made in what the staff called "interpretation." Visitors were told about the stat-

Visitors enjoy a magnificent view from Liberty's crown windows.

Bedloe's Island with (A) staff housing, (B) administration building, (C) restaurant and gift shop, and (D) statue. The four buildings on the far side of the island are army housing yet to be removed.

ue's beginnings and her significance through the years by means of tours, movies, exhibits, and printed matter, and school children were entertained and informed through special programs and puppet shows.

By November 1954 the number of immigrants coming into the country was only a handful, and the facilities at Ellis Island were shut down. The Immigration Service offices moved back to lower Manhattan, and the federal government then tried to sell the island. No one seemed interested. There were about fifty different proposals submitted for the island during the late 1950s and early 1960s, but for one reason or another none of them worked out. Among them were suggestions for a drug rehabilitation center, a women's prison, a home for the aged, a college, a gambling casino, and even a golf course. In the end, nothing was done with the thirty-five buildings occupying Ellis Island, and gradually they were ravaged by neglect and vandalism.

In 1955, probably partly to keep the memory of Ellis Island alive, the Secretary of Interior signed a cooperative agreement with the American Museum of Immigration, Inc. Fund-raising efforts were then launched and continued for the next decade.

As the 1950s came to a close, considerable money had been raised to build the new American Museum of Immigration and many of its materials had been gathered. In addition, the rubble from the old army days was gone. The administration and concession buildings were finished and in use. Liberty had staff members living in their new quarters, and most of the grounds had been landscaped. The entire green tree-filled island would have made Auguste Bartholdi proud.

13 THE TROUBLED SIXTIES

As the 1960s began, a very fragile peace existed in the world. Both Russia and the United States had added atomic weapons to their defenses, and other countries soon followed their example.

The United States had emerged from World War II as a world leader and wanted very much to be looked upon as a peaceful world power. Some people thought the eagle, a strong, carnivorous bird, stood more for subjugation than freedom. They argued that Liberty was widely known and cherished as a true symbol of America's hospitality to all creeds and races. Liberty, far better than the eagle, they said, displayed our beliefs to the rest of the world.

Liberty, however, did not succeed in becoming the official national symbol, but she did achieve having her island named for her. On June 30, 1960, Bedloe's Island was officially renamed Liberty Island.

In 1961 over 750,000 visitors made the trip to Liberty Island. They came from all over the country and all over the world, with only 10 percent coming from New York City. The following year a record-setting 172,052 visitors came to see Liberty during the month of July alone.

Because of the increased traffic to Liberty Island and because some New Jersey citizens had always felt Bedloe's Island should belong to them, a Congressman from New Jersey proposed in October of 1962 building a footbridge between Liberty Island and New Jersey, which he said would eliminate the problem of reaching the island from traffic-clogged lower Manhattan streets. The proposal was studied and eventually turned down by the Secretary of the Interior, Stewart Udall. He said a footbridge or causeway would "destroy the scenic character of the island and detract from the present dignity and impressiveness of the Statue of Liberty."

Later that month, on October 28, 1962, Liberty's seventy-sixth birthday was celebrated, highlighted by the laying of the cornerstone of the American Museum of Immigration. It was hoped that the musem would be completed in time for the 1964 World's Fair to take place in New York.

By the mid-sixties the people of the United States were increasingly alarmed about events taking place in other countries around the world and concerned about the way their government was dealing with them. It was a time when young people, in particular, were very vocal in voicing their protests.

An island country not far from the nation's shores, Cuba, had a pro-Communist government headed by Fidel Castro. When he allowed Russian missiles to be placed on the island, it appeared that the two great world powers were on the brink of war. Fortunately, an agreement was reached between President Kennedy and Soviet Premier Khrushchev, and the Soviet missile bases were dismantled. It also looked as if the United States might be drawn into small, unpopular wars being fought on the other side of the world.

Since the Statue of Liberty stood for liberty and freedom, was a popular monument, and was located next to the country's largest city, she was often chosen as a place to stage protests. The National Park Service staff members at Liberty Island were sympathetic to protesters who wanted to stage legal demonstrations at Liberty Island. If notified of a demonstration (as was required), they provided a loudspeaker system, a place to meet, and any other assistance they could reasonably give. However, frequently illegal demonstrations attracted much more attention than legal ones, and Liberty, throughout her history, has been subjected to some pretty humiliating and sometimes dangerous demonstrations. At no time in her history did this occur more than in the late 1960s and early 1970s.

On January 3, 1965, nineteen Cuban exiles marked the sixth anniversary of Fidel Castro's rise to power by chaining themselves together on the balcony at Liberty's feet, which is ten stories from the ground. They were linked wrist to wrist with handcuffs, padlocks, and lengths of half-inch chain. Before locking themselves together, they unfurled a huge pro-Castro flag. When park officials asked them to unlock themselves, their spokesman said, "We threw the keys away."

Park officials had to go look for a bolt cutter, which they used to snip the chains. The exiles were then taken in the elevator to the ground level. In an effort to be as considerate as possible, park officials gave the exiles hot drinks before putting them on a ferry back to Manhattan. There were no charges against them because there was no property damage.

There were some plans for demonstrations, however, that were of a far more violent nature. Also in January of 1965, another group, composed of a small number of black extremists, felt they did not get the freedoms they deserved in the United States. They were so angry, in fact, that they decided to blow up America's most famous democratic symbols—the Washington Monument, the Liberty Bell, and the Statue of Liberty.

One member of the gang went out to Liberty Island on a cold day in early January. He climbed the stairs to the crown, and when he left, he bought a small model of Liberty. He wanted to use the model to show to his friends and work out the details of a crazy scheme. The plan was to break the lock on the door leading to the upraised arm—the one that holds the flame aloft—and plant dynamite there. The gang hoped to use enough dynamite to blow off Liberty's head and arm.

Somehow government officials found out about the plot and put a stop to it on the day it was to take place, February 16, 1965. Explosive experts found thirty sticks of dynamite in a car in Riverdale, New York, only a few miles from New York harbor. Suspects were also arrested in the area of the Washington Monument in Washington, D.C., and the Liberty Bell in Philadelphia. After this scare more security guards were assigned to each of the monuments.

The threats to the statue and the unsettled times, however, did not put a stop to the improvements being made to Liberty Island. Work on the American Museum of Immigration continued, but because of funding and construction difficulties the museum was not ready for the 1964 World's Fair.

An important event did take place, however, on May 11, 1965, when President Lyndon Baines Johnson came to Liberty Island to announce that Ellis Island was to be made a part of the Statue of Liberty National Monument and would also be under the supervision of the National Park Service.

On the same day as the Ellis Island announcement, President Johnson, standing at the base of the pedestal, made a speech in which he asked Congress to pass an immigration bill that would abolish the national quota restrictions set up in the 1920s following World War I. President Johnson wanted to admit newcomers on the basis of their skills rather than just their nationalities. On October 3, 1965, Congress made the immigration changes advocated by President Johnson and his predecessor, John F. Kennedy. The legislation allowed thousands of newcomers to enter the country who had previously been excluded.

At a party one evening, soon after the Ellis Island announcement, Secretary of the Interior Stewart Udall was talking to the famous American architect Philip Johnson. Secretary Udall admitted he did not know what to do with Ellis Island and asked the architect to come up with a plan.

Johnson did not think there were very many buildings worth saving and suggested demolishing all of them except for the main immigration building and a hospital. The entire island would then be made into a recreational park. The primary feature of Johnson's plan was a new monument to be built on the southwestern part of the island. It was to be a 130-foot-high circular wall to be called the "Wall of the 16 Million" to represent the immigrants who passed through Ellis Island. Visitors

would be able to walk up exterior spiraling ramps and read the names of their ancestors listed on wall plaques. Johnson's proposal was loved by some and abhorred by others. Those who didn't like it thought the monument looked a little too much like a football stadium. Philip Johnson submitted his proposal to the federal government, but he never received a reply. Ellis Island was once more forgotten, and the buildings and grounds continued to deteriorate.

There were very few dull moments for Liberty, however, during the turbulent 1960s. November 9, 1965, started out like any other ordinary, action-packed day in New York City, but late in the afternoon the city came to almost a total halt when the largest power failure in history blacked out all of New York City and parts of nine northeastern states.

Office workers were stranded in skyscrapers because elevators weren't working. Some walked down fifty or more flights of stairs to get to ground level. The subways stopped running, and traffic on the street was in chaos because there were no traffic lights. But the strangest sight of all was the inky blackness of the city usually brilliant with millions of lights. It was then that the residents of lower Manhattan saw a comforting sight—the floodlit figure of Liberty and her glowing torch. Except for an occasional passing boat, the statue provided the only beam of light in the harbor. Liberty was able to remain bathed in light because power for her system was supplied by a New Jersey power company.

Six months later, on May 22, 1966, possibly motivated by New Jersey's ability to keep Liberty's lights on during the blackout, a band of fifty-five New Jersey businessmen took over Liberty Island following an intensive campaign by the Chamber of Commerce claiming once again that by geographic rights the

President Lyndon B. Johnson, Vice President Hubert Humphrey, their wives, and other important officials arrive by helicopter to announce that Ellis Island will become a part of the Statue of Liberty National Monument.

island belonged to New Jersey. The National Park Service cheerfully allowed the businessmen to take over for a day but stood firm in its refusal to give the island to New Jersey.

The businessmen also wanted ferry service between New Jersey and Liberty Island—which they later succeeded in getting. A request for New Jersey postmarks on island mail, however, was denied. After the New Jersey demonstrators were served box lunches on the island lawn, they boarded a ferry for Manhattan and drove back to New Jersey.

As the 1960s came to a close, there were four National Park Service families living on the residential end of the island with a total of nine children from toddlers to teenagers. Asked how they liked living there, the older children complained because it was difficult for them to see their friends since they could not go into the city at night.

Most of the children went to school on Governor's Island, a forty-five-minute ferry ride during the course of which they had to change ferries in Manhattan. Sometimes, though, they were taken to school quickly on the island motor launch.

There were some good things about being a child on Liberty Island, however. Liberty's torch was closed to the public, but the island children were sometimes permitted to go up into it. They had backyards with magnificent views, and they could fish from them.

Most National Park Service employees, however, considered being assigned to Liberty Island a hardship duty. They had joined the Park Service because they wanted to live with nature in the wild and wanted no part of a National Monument that was so close to New York City. In addition, on Liberty Island they knew they would be affected by the high cost of city living while being isolated from the advantages the city had to offer. They felt having to pay $35 a month for housing was much too expensive. Most of them really had the country mouse's aversion

The lights of the Statue of Liberty and New York City on a typical night

to city life, and they didn't feel living on an island would keep out the evil ways of the city. It was also dangerous at times to live at the foot of such a popular and important monument. Nevertheless, whatever the general feelings of Park Service employees were toward being assigned to Liberty Island, once they were there, for the most part, officials and their families grew to have very strong positive or negative reactions to the island and the statue.

The New York Times ran a story on December 19, 1969, about a forest ranger named Pingree Crawford. He, his wife, Judy, and their two children watched as a moving van—brought to the island by a derrick and a barge—came to pick up their possessions and move them to their next post, an Indian archaeological site in rural Georgia. Pingree Crawford had spent two years being second in command at the statue, and he knew he would miss his life there. He had enjoyed going to sleep at night with the soothing toll of bell buoys and an occasional foghorn. He would miss the sycamore trees growing outside his front door and the breathtaking view of the New York skyline.

When asked how he felt about living on Liberty Island, Mr. Crawford admitted life near the statue stirred up a lot of emotions. "You listen to what people say and you can't help being moved," he said. "Particularly when you see foreigners standing near the statue and looking at it and weeping."

Mr. Crawford went on to tell about the two or three times a week he had gone up into the torch at night. "You know no one is allowed in the torch at any time," he reminded the reporter. "But I used to go there alone and just stand there looking at the city. It's the greatest city in the world." New York City and the statue had worked their magic on Pingree Crawford, and he probably would not forget them.

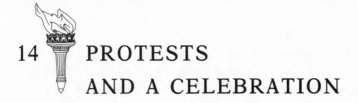

14 PROTESTS
AND A CELEBRATION

The first event regarding Liberty to make the news-paper headlines in the 1970s was another attempt by New Jersey to get its share of the statue. This time a New Jersey legislator asked that Liberty be mounted on a swivel so that New Jersey residents could get a front view of her once in a while. "She is a symbol of freedom," the New Jersey congressman said. "And she deserves our full admiration." Needless to say, the request was turned down.

During the 1970s the Statue of Liberty continued to be plagued with illegal protests and occupations. On December 26, 1971, a band of sixteen antiwar veterans seized control of the statue and vowed to stay there until New Year's Eve as a protest against the continuing war in Vietnam. They promised they would re-spect the statue property and not do anything violent, but they would not come out until they had made their point.

The takeover began when the veterans mingled with the tour-ists and then hid in the basement when the last visitors left on the 5:00 P.M. ferry. Two hours later they threw out a night watchman when he discovered them. They barricaded them-selves inside by blocking all three entrances to the basement with huge beams left over from an interior renovation project.

When it got dark, the veterans climbed up to the crown and hung an upside-down American flag as a symbol of the distress they felt about the war. It was lighted by the crown lights.

Later that night they broke through the door to the upraised arm and climbed the ladder to the torch, where they hung another upside-down flag.

The protesters broke into the statue's food concession, but they very considerately left money for the food they took. Twenty-two National Park guards surrounded the statue while a Coast Guard cutter and a police launch circled the island all night. No attempt was made to evict the squatters during the hours of darkness.

The invaders held the statue for forty-two hours before they were finally talked into coming out, and they emerged with their clenched fists held high in the air. They felt it was quite an achievement to have occupied Liberty for a longer period of time than had ever been achieved in previous takeover protests. They were even more thrilled when they learned there would be no arrests.

They were also delighted by the amount of publicity they felt their cause had attracted. The story of the takeover had appeared on the first pages of many of the nation's newspapers, and some of the veterans appeared on the "Today" and "Dick Cavett" television programs.

In 1972 the American Museum of Immigration was finally opened to the public. The country was getting ready for its Bicentennial celebration on July 4, 1976, and wanted to focus interest on its rich and varied past.

In the years of preparation for the nation's two hundredth birthday, the statue continued to be troubled with illegal demonstrations. On June 3, 1972, fourteen members of an anti-Castro group handcuffed themselves to iron railings inside the pedestal. Two years later, on April 19, 1974, twenty-one college youths barricaded themselves inside the statue and vowed to remain until President Richard Nixon left his job as President of the United States. Both groups were considerate of statue property. In fact, the protesters brought their own food with them. The anti-Nixon youths spent the night in the statue and left at 6:45 A.M. the following morning when park officials read a court order evicting them as trespassers. No arrests were made.

These demonstrations did not, however, get in the way of plans for the biggest birthday party ever held in the United States—plans that of course included the country's most popular female symbol. To make the statue brighter than ever, it was proposed that once again Liberty should have a new lighting system. The last major one had been installed in 1931, and since then enormous strides had been made in lighting technology.

Two years before the celebration, Crouse Hinds, a Syracuse electrical company, designed Liberty's new lighting system. The firm expected to be paid by the federal government for the project, but when funds were not provided, Crouse Hinds decided to donate the new lights.

The new system provided four times the illumination of the 1931 version and could be run for one-third the cost. More light for less money was possible because of new low-energy technology and advanced lighting techniques.

High-pressure sodium lamps, rich in yellow hues, were installed in the torch. New mercury lamps in the crown provided a blue-green jeweled effect. Metal halide lamps were directed at the statue and bathed Liberty in a strong white light. The pedestal was illuminated with a blend of white halides and yellow sodium lights.

Plans for a choreographed, push-button, and electronically controlled fireworks display to explode over New York harbor for half an hour on the night July 4, 1976, were also in the works two years before the actual celebration. More than 3,000 shells would be shot off in what promoters hoped would be the most widely viewed fireworks display in history. Macy's Department Store in New York City arranged the fireworks show and hired experts from the Walt Disney organization to help with the planning.

The Statue of Liberty was to be in the center of the display. The fireworks would be set off from Liberty, Ellis, and Governor's islands and from three barges in the harbor. The controls would be located on top of the World Trade Center.

Another exciting aspect of the Bicentennial celebration was

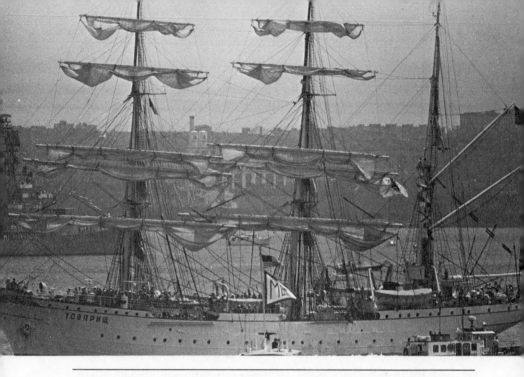

The tall ships came to New York harbor to help celebrate the nation's one hundredth birthday on July 4, 1976.

a parade of the old-fashioned tall ships in New York harbor. They would remind New Yorkers of another era.

Finally the big day arrived. It was a typically hot, sunny July 4. For days the tall ships had been arriving; on the Fourth there were more than 200 high-masted sailing ships around New York. There were also visiting warships from twenty-two nations, who exchanged frequent cannon salutes as they glided past each other. An estimated 30,000 small boats cruised around the larger boats for closer looks, and the Coast Guard considered it a miracle that there were no major water collisions. Party-goers jammed balconies along the shoreline to wave at the passing ships. Sailors, many perched high in riggings, waved back.

Shortly after sunset the Mayor of New York threw the switch to bathe the Statue of Liberty in her powerful new lights. Thirteen searchlights each weighing 2½ tons slowly played around Liberty's crowned head.

As the fireworks began, huge crowds formed a human carpet

across the southern tip of Manhattan, covering parks, sidewalks, and curbs. Spectators were also perched on balconies, rooftops, window ledges, and automobile roofs and hoods. Most brought radios because the show included music and a commentary. An estimated 6,000,000 people watched from the shore, and millions more across the land watched on their television sets.

After the last bursts of color showered down from the sky above Liberty, Ellis, and Governor's islands, there was a moment of silence as all eyes turned toward the radiant lady in the harbor. As a helicopter towed a flag of red, white, and blue lights, sixty by one hundred feet, across the night sky over the head of Liberty, all 6,000,000 spectators, many with tears in their eyes, joined in the singing of "The Star Spangled Banner." It was very much an American-style spectacle, and the Statue of Liberty was in the center of it all.

The winter after the Bicentennial celebration, a new superintendent and his family moved onto Liberty Island. According to a story in *Esquire* magazine, Dave Moffitt, his wife Carolyn, and their three children, Michael, seven, John, eleven, and Andrea, thirteen, arrived on a bitterly cold January day. The Moffitts trudged through the fresh snow and, after introducing themselves to their neighbors, settled into their island home. The family soon joined a church in Manhattan, where Carolyn sang in the choir. The boys searched the island for driftwood and built a backyard clubhouse. Andrea sketched the island's gulls. In his spare time Dave Moffitt fished for striped bass from the seawall at the end of his yard.

The Moffitts had a fairly quiet first month, but then things began to happen. On February 16, 1977, a police boat picked up the children from their school on Governor's Island because the regular ferry service had been stopped. Six Iranian students were protesting because they didn't feel their countrymen in Iran were being treated fairly. The demonstrators had climbed the steps to Liberty's crown and smashed seven glass window panes in order to hang out five-yard-long banners reading, FREE THE 18 and DOWN WITH THE SHAH.

When Dave Moffitt climbed the 171 steps in the statue to talk to the young Iranians, he found that six students had chained themselves together inside the head of Liberty. They demanded the superintendent provide a televised press conference in the crown. Dave Moffitt refused, trying to explain it would be very difficult to haul television equipment up the long, winding stairway. Angered at being turned down, the Iranians ordered Mr. Moffitt to leave.

Eight hours later, the park rangers cut the protesters' chains, and the students left peacefully. They were not arrested because they had surrendered, and they agreed to pay for the repair of the broken windows.

After the demonstration was over, the Moffitts talked about their day. Dave Moffitt felt bad because thousands of sightseers had been turned away during the hours the ferry service was discontinued. Carolyn was annoyed by the swarms of reporters overrunning the island. As for the boys, they put up a sign on their clubhouse reading: KEEP OUT.

The Moffitts soon learned that the island that was their home attracted visitors from all over the world and some protesters who were peaceful and well behaved, as well as others who were destructive, violent, and more than a little offbeat. Life on Liberty Island was seldom boring.

One man thought President Jimmy Carter's agents were trying to poison him. He wrapped himself in an American flag and lay down in the crown. On another day there was much confusion in the crown area because a Puerto Rican group of protesters tried to take over the space at the same time that a camera crew was shooting a movie starring Elliott Gould and a boxing kangaroo.

One of the most dramatic takeovers occurred as the decade of the 1970s came to a close. There was a great deal of tension in the United States at the time regarding the nation's troubled

Iranian students hang banners over the face of the Statue of Liberty during a protest on February 16, 1977.

relationship with the oil-rich country of Iran. Under the leadership of the Shah of Iran, who had been a friend to the United States, the nation prospered, but to many people in his own country he was regarded as unfair and cruel. He was finally removed from office and, as a sick, aging old man, traveled to New York City for gall bladder surgery. He also had cancer, and it seemed likely he might spend up to a year in the United States receiving medical treatment.

Some Iranian students in the United States, many of whom had left Iran to get away from the Shah, were angry that the United States had allowed the Shah to come to America. They thought no matter how sick he was, he ought to be sent back to Iran to be tried and punished.

One Sunday early in November of 1979, while the Shah was recuperating in New York Hospital and Dave Moffitt was attending church in Manhattan with his family, a group of Iranian students took the ferry out to the statue and climbed to the crown. Soon a 140-foot-long banner reading, SHAH MUST BE TRIED AND PUNISHED, fluttered from Liberty's windows. Then the seven protesters chained themselves to railings inside the statue.

When Dave Moffitt received the news, he immediately drove to the tip of Manhattan, where a staff boat was waiting for him. The first thing he did was order the statue closed. Two hours later park officials cut the protesters' chains, put them in handcuffs, and led them to Dave Moffitt's office.

The Iranians complained about their handcuffs and about allowing the Shah to come to the United States for surgery. At one point the protesters, who were Muslims, asked if they could go outside and kneel toward their religious city, Mecca. Mr. Moffitt said, "Fine," but changed his mind when he saw a hoard of cameramen outside on the lawn. He did not want to give the Iranians the publicity they were so anxious to have.

At about this time a call came from Washington saying that a few hours earlier the United States embassy at Tehran had been captured by a group of Iranians, and many Americans were

Superintendent Dave Moffitt holds a press conference.

being held as hostages. Officials in Washington warned Dave Moffitt to be careful because there might be a connection between the Iranians on Liberty Island and the kidnappers in Tehran.

Dave Moffitt ordinarily would have given the protesters some coffee and sent them home after delivering a stern lecture. This time, however, it was felt some punishment was deserved. The Iranian students were fined, and their passports were taken from them. Many people felt they should have been sent back to Iran.

There was no denying that the 1960s and 1970s were troubled times for the United States and were often dangerous times for the lady on Liberty Island. The nation's Bicentennial celebration, however, had been a grand, happy affair, and Liberty could now begin to look forward hopefully to better times and her own one hundredth birthday.

15 A CLIMB LEADS
TO RESTORATION PLANS

On a sunny Saturday morning in early May 1980, which just happened also to be the Mother's Day weekend, two men carrying climbing gear and backpacks boarded the 9:00 A.M. ferry to the Statue of Liberty. They were thirty-five-year-old British-born Edwin Drummond, an experienced mountain climber, and a thirty-one-year-old house painter from San Francisco, Steven Rutherford, who was only a beginning climber. Once on the island, Drummond and Rutherford entered the pedestal and took the elevator to the balcony at the base of the statue. There they put on their climbing equipment, including placing special mountain-climbing suction cups on their boots. Then they proceeded to climb up the base and onto Liberty's right foot.

Rutherford got as far as Liberty's right knee and stayed there while his more experienced partner continued to climb. It was not easy. Very soon there were a great many policemen and park rangers, including Superintendent Moffitt, shouting from the balcony. Thousands of other spectators watched from the ground level. Drummond tried to concentrate on the tricky and dangerous business of scaling the thin green copper skin. He pumped furiously on one rubber suction cup, then the other, but they did not seem to stick for more than thirty seconds.

The noise alone must have unnerved the climbers. Police and rangers used bull horns to order them to come down, helicopters circled close to the statue, and someone inside the statue was banging at them. Drummond slipped twice but each time caught himself.

By midafternoon Drummond had reached a point between the statue's shoulder blades. To support himself, he jammed two climbing nuts into a fold of Liberty's gown. Dave Moffitt, watching Drummond's forceful arm movements from his office window, voiced to a reporter his fear that they were hammering in pitons.

The more he watched, the more Dave Moffitt was convinced that the climbers were doing serious damage to the statue by driving into the penny-thick copper sheating steel spikes with eyeholes through which ropes could be pulled. He also told reporters that rivets were being knocked loose and that in some places the copper metal sheets had been folded back.

Spectators on the ground shared Dave Moffitt's impression of the damage being done. They joined the police and rangers in shouting ever louder orders to come down. "I hope you break your necks," some angry tourists yelled up at the climbers.

In spite of his fears about the injuries being inflicted on the thin-skinned statue, Superintendent Moffitt would not allow anyone to forcibly remove the two men. He said there was no way to stop them until they fell off or reached the top.

When Drummond got to a point where his footing was fairly secure, he unfurled a twenty-five-foot-long white banner with red letters that read: LIBERTY WAS FRAMED: FREE GERONIMO PRATT. The banner referred to Elmer Pratt, a member of a group who called themselves the Black Panthers party. In 1972 Pratt had been convicted and given a life sentence for killing a school teacher during a robbery on a tennis court in California. Most observers at the statue had never heard of Elmer Pratt.

The two climbers believed that the Federal Bureau of Investigation had brought about his conviction by questionable tactics. They had been influenced by Amnesty International's worldwide efforts on behalf of many people unjustly deprived of their civil rights. Edwin Drummond was an experienced international protest climber. He had climbed the Nelson Monument in London, England, to dramatize his feelings about South Africa's racial politics, and he had scaled San Francisco's Grace Cathedral, where he spent the night in defense of Pratt.

At 5:00 P.M. the police cleared the area of about 1,000 tourists and sent them home on the last ferries of the day. Dave Moffitt pleaded with the climbers to come down and offered to leave the lighted banner up all night. Even though it was getting very cold, the climbers insisted upon spending the night on the statue. By this time Drummond had climbed down to Rutherford's level, and the pair opened up sleeping bags on a horizontal fold of Liberty's gown and ate the food they had brought with them. Park rangers placed large air-filled bags below the two men to cushion them against a possible fall during the long hours of darkness.

Off and on throughout the long night, the climbers recited poems by Emerson, Sandburg, and Auden. With thousands of watts of halide floodlights directed at them, it was almost impossible to sleep. In their homes nearby, the Moffitts and the other park ranger families also got very little sleep. All night helicopters circled over the little island.

At 5:00 A.M., the climbers, asleep at last, were awakened by a ranger using a bull horn. A few hours later the pair carefully broke camp and descended to the foot of the statue, where they were met by a crowd of rangers, policemen, reporters, and photographers. This time the protesters were promptly arrested for criminal trespass and damaging government property.

Dave Moffitt tried to whisk the two men away quickly from the scribbling reporters. He felt the protesters had already received plenty of publicity. Drummond, however, managed to gain enough time to deny having caused any damage to the

---

Statue climber Edwin Drummond unfurls a long white banner reading, LIBERTY WAS FRAMED: FREE GERONIMO PRATT.

statue. He claimed to be a "rock climber" who does not use steel pitons. He said all of his climbing had been done with special rock-climbing suction cups attached to his shoes, and he escaped from his captors long enough to give a brief climbing demonstration on the statue base.

Dave Moffitt, on the other hand, was still sure the damage was serious and would be costly to repair. An inside inspection had revealed that about fifteen rivets had possibly been removed so that spikes could be put in rivet holes. The superintendent also said that Drummond had removed protective tar from some of the seams between the copper-surface plates. The purpose of the tar was to keep winds and rain out of the statue and to hold the plates in place.

Worst of all, even if the climbers had caused no damage at all, the cost of erecting scaffolding and sending inspectors up to look would be about $80,000. The city, alarmed that scaling the statue was even possible, decided to spend an extra $20,000 for policemen, police boats, and helicopters to beef up the protection provided by the park rangers.

The National Park Service did not waste any time. During the following week they erected a four-deck scaffold beginning at the tenth floor observation balcony, which would allow experts to carefully examine at least a small part of the statue's skin. The weekend after Mother's Day the inspection team gathered on the balcony and began their work.

One inspector, Edward McManus, an architectural conservator working for the National Park Service, told reporters, "Our concern is twofold. First we want to determine the extent of the damage caused by the climb, and second this is a good point to determine whether the patina is stable or corroding."

It was feared the patina might be deteriorating. It was well known that the statue's environment had become increasingly hostile. Coal-burning plants, largely along the nearby New Jersey shore, were spewing out oxides of sulphur and nitrogen, which when combined with moisture caused harmful acid rains to fall upon the harbor and the statue.

As soon as he climbed the scaffold, Mr. McManus requested his scalpel. Very delicately he skimmed the scalpel over Liberty's skin, removing some dustlike particles into a black plastic container. After several careful scrapings the professor nodded. "I think that will do," he said.

The particles were taken to a science laboratory to be studied and x-rayed. The inspectors doing the job were amazed that this was the first time in almost a hundred years that Liberty's green skin was going to receive a thorough chemical examination.

After climbing around on the scaffold and peering closely at Liberty's shell, the specialists announced that the climbers did not punch holes with spikes as park officials had believed. The holes had probably been caused by corrosion.

It soon became clear that any damage done by the climbers was nothing compared to the problems caused by acid rain, previous harmful renovations, neglect, vandalism, and time itself. Professor Norman Weiss, a member of the Columbia School of Architecture, spoke for all the inspectors and other National Park Service officials when he suggested, "Maybe this is the time to itemize problems with the statue. It's not like a building where you can do a little maintenance now and a little later. It will require a major investment of personnel and dollars."

The National Park Service then asked a firm of French engineers led by Philippe Grandjean, who was an authority on Gustave Eiffel's work, to make a more thorough study. The French firm confirmed the findings of the National Park Service and stated that if immediate steps were not taken, Liberty's skin and armature might collapse.

The engineers and various friends of the statue were called together by Philipe Vallery-Radot, who was the grandson of the great scientist Louis Pasteur. A formal organization, called the French-American Committee for Restoration of the Statue of Liberty, was set up to expand upon the study done by Philippe Grandjean and to present proposals for restoration. Over the years, as Liberty became more and more an all-American symbol, it seemed as though the French connection had almost been forgotten, but as her one hundredth birthday approached and she needed help, the French reminded the Americans that the statue had started out as a symbol of belief in liberty shared by the two countries. At this point the Americans were glad to have the help of expert French engineers and architects, and Philippe Grandjean was put in charge of the study and worked closely with the National Park Service. The results were published in a lavishly illustrated *Statue of Liberty Architectural and Engineering Report*, which was made available to the public.

The study made of the outside of Liberty's skin revealed that Liberty was several shades of green, and there were dark stains in many places. Though the committee was not particularly concerned about the varying shades of green, several explanations were given. When the copper sheets were manufactured for Bartholdi, the amounts of impurities in each sheet varied, and these different amounts caused the sheets to weather in varying ways. Also the statue was dirtier in some places than in others. There were accumulations of dirt in folds of her gown and in other parts of the statue not directly washed by falling rain, such as under her nose and chin. Acid rains had corroded some areas more than others.

The dark stains were caused mostly by coal tar leaking out from the places where the copper plates were joined together. There were also some green stains on the granite pedestal, caused by copper sulfate solutions dribbling down the statue and forming deposits on the base.

To the great relief of the committee, they found that the thickness of the skin had remained the same over the years. It was decided that no more needed to be done to Liberty's skin than some light washing. No one wanted to disturb the patina that had protected the lady so well through the years.

Some of Liberty's 300 copper plates, which were either structurally or visually unacceptable, needed to be replaced. The new plates were to be as close as possible to the original plates, and a method to speed up the oxidation process would have to be devised so that the new plates would match the old plates in color.

The architects also found that there were no major flaws in the main structure. The design of the pylon and secondary structures had stood up well to the test of time.

The committee decided, however, that this would be a good time to make some improvements in the interior so that visiting the statue would be a more pleasant experience. Auguste Bartholdi had never intended that visitors come inside his statue. The narrow and steep 171-step spiral staircase running from the base to the crown was intended only for workmen. He would have been amazed to learn that by the 1980s as many as 2,500 people a day climbed the dangerous and inadequate stairs in often brutal conditions.

There had never been any attempt to control the interior environment of Liberty. In the summer heat it was suffocating inside the statue, especially during the peak hours. Temperatures on hot days hovered around 110° F (44° C). The humidity also was often unbearable, and when the statue was crowded, the carbon-dioxide levels exceeded acceptable limits. Having an envelope that was not watertight resulted in additional humidity and condensation problems. Sound levels were also uncomfortably high when Liberty was crowded. In the winter the statue was heated only by radiators, and the heat escaped through the many small holes in the skin. Air flowing naturally from the bottom to the top was the only ventilation.

Making improvements for visitors had always been done in a piecemeal fashion without an overall, long-range plan. On numerous occasions the interior skin and armature had been painted to cover up corroded sections and graffiti, and there were probably as many as six layers of paint on the interior. When the old paint began to peel and new paint was put on top, moisture was trapped between the layers and further corrosion began taking place.

The committee's plans for upgrading the interior were ambitious. The old stairway would be widened and repaired and

The old staircase from the pedestal to the crown area shows signs of being heavily used.

new, safer railings added. The rest platforms along the way would also be improved. The old wire mesh would be taken down and replaced with something that would permit views of the entire interior of the statue. The layers of old paint and coal tar would be removed and the lighting improved. A new double-decker elevator would be installed in the pedestal.

The committee recommended that air conditioning and a new system of ventilation be installed. In order to do these two things, however, it was necessary to make the statue more weather-resistant and hopefully watertight. Workers would close all of the seams with a sealant and plug the numerous holes with a type of copper called touch-pitch, which would duplicate the less pure metal of Bartholdi's day.

The major problem the committee faced, however, was the serious deterioration of Liberty's skeleton known as the armature. It was almost totally rusted away! Eiffel's brilliant scheme of protecting the iron skeleton from the copper skin had failed, and the culprit was ordinary water. Far more of it had gotten into the statue than Eiffel had ever dreamed was possible. There were, the committee found, many causes for the water damage.

First of all, there were thousands of unused rivet holes all over the statue. Every time it rained or was foggy, moisture entered the statue through these holes.

Second, there was a large hole punched in Liberty's upraised right arm by one of the rays in her crown, and moisture was able to enter the statue in large amounts through this hole.

The dark band in the middle of this picture shows an iron rib that has almost totally rusted away. The pieces with three bolts are saddles and are attached to the skin. The ribs (or armature) pass through the saddles and are not directly attached to the copper skin.

Bartholdi had never intended that the ray come in contact with the torch arm. The problem occurred because Liberty's head and upraised arm had been mounted incorrectly almost one hundred years earlier. Since the weight of the arm was not carried directly to the pylon, the arm had weakened over the years. Then the Black Tom munitions explosion in 1916 caused further weakening and shifting of the arm. During heavy winds the arm actually swung slightly in the air. There was some thought of removing the upraised arm and head and putting them on correctly, but it was decided that the operation would be too costly and complicated. The arm would simply be reinforced in some way and the hole mended.

The third major cause of water damage, which was by far the most serious one, was the result of America's love affair with electricity. Bartholdi had designed the statue before the invention of the light bulb. Therefore, the original torch had no openings in it, and Bartholdi had hoped it would eventually be gilded with gold.

As soon as the Americans got hold of the statue, however, they began punching holes in the torch in order to make the light shine from it. Finally in 1916 it was almost completely glassed in when Gutzon Borglum created a design that cut away so many pieces of copper that the torch looked like a huge Tiffany lamp. The problem was that no one anticipated the kind of beating the torch would receive from the weather as it stood unprotected high in the air over the harbor. The glass plates proved not to be adequately sealed. Eventually whenever it rained, there was a small flood running down the upraised arm and into the statue.

As a result of the great amount of water that had entered the statue over the years, as well as the damage caused by the salty environment, acid rain, and the carbon-dioxide build-up inside

The Borglum torch with Ellis Island to the left and the World Trade Center towers and Manhattan directly behind the statue

the statue, the asbestos strips covered with shellac that had so carefully been inserted by workmen in 1885 had disintegrated. The excessive moisture created a conductor that speeded up the electrolytic destruction in every place where iron met copper. Many of the 1,500 ribs, being made of the inferior metal, had become badly corroded, causing them to expand, flake, and pull on the copper saddles attaching them to the skin. The committee inspectors found that a third of the saddles and their rivets had partly or totally pulled away from the copper skin, leaving gaping holes in the metal.

Probably taking a very deep breath, the committee decided they had no other choice but to replace almost every one of the 1,500 ribs in the statue. The only old pieces of the original armature that would be permitted to remain would be those in the right foot. They were to be left alone so that future generations could see in-place examples of the original armature.

To put a stop to future corrosion of the armature, a new material called "316-L" was selected to replace the iron. This is a low-carbon stainless steel, which was chosen for its rust-resistant properties. Compared with other alloys studied, "316-L" is easier to bend, and therefore using it would make it less difficult to duplicate the many complicated shapes in the armature.

The original ribs, all of them different, had been hammered into shape by blacksmiths, who crafted them by following the curves in Liberty's copper skin. The wooden molds might have been useful for recreating the 1,500 individual ribs, but they no longer existed, and Eiffel's detailed engineering drawings were destroyed by a fire in his suburban Paris office in the early 1900s.

All the ribs obviously could not be removed at one time or the statue's copper envelope would sag and fall. The only possible way was to remove them a few at a time along with their

---

This photograph of the statue's interior reveals a complicated system of curved ribs as they follow the shape of Liberty's gown.

saddles. The ribs would then be duplicated in the new material by using the original ribs as patterns. The most intricate ribs would have to be heated and fitted into place while they were still flexible enough to be bent and twisted. Teflon would be added to the ribs where they passed through the saddles to ensure that the ribs would be able to move freely.

The committee also planned to replace all the flat iron bars that connected the armature to the statue's secondary framework. For this project they chose a less malleable stainless steel called "Ferralium 225," the stiffer quality of which, they felt, made it ideal for handling the stress between the armature and the secondary frame.

The committee also decided that the torch was beyond repair and needed to be replaced—the second biggest project of the restoration. They felt it would be best for the beauty of the statue, and certainly for stopping the leaking problem, to return to Bartholdi's original design. The plan called for a torch covered with copper sheathing containing no openings and gilded with gold. It would be lit from the outside. The new torch was to be constructed in a shed erected at the foot of the statue so that visitors might watch it being built.

The first order of business for the restoration would be to remove all the layers of paint and coal tar from the interior skin. Removal was necessary in order to repair the skin and armature, to eliminate pockets of condensation, to restore the copper to its original state, and to make inspection and maintenance easier.

The committee examined several methods, many of them quite exciting and adventurous. Among them were sandblasting, solvent cleaning, carbo-ice cleaning, high-pressure water jets, hot-air guns, and even bombarding the paint build-up with bits of hard nutshells.

Liberty's face is clearly shown in reverse in this interior photo showing repair work to be done. Compare this photograph with the early engraving on page 53.

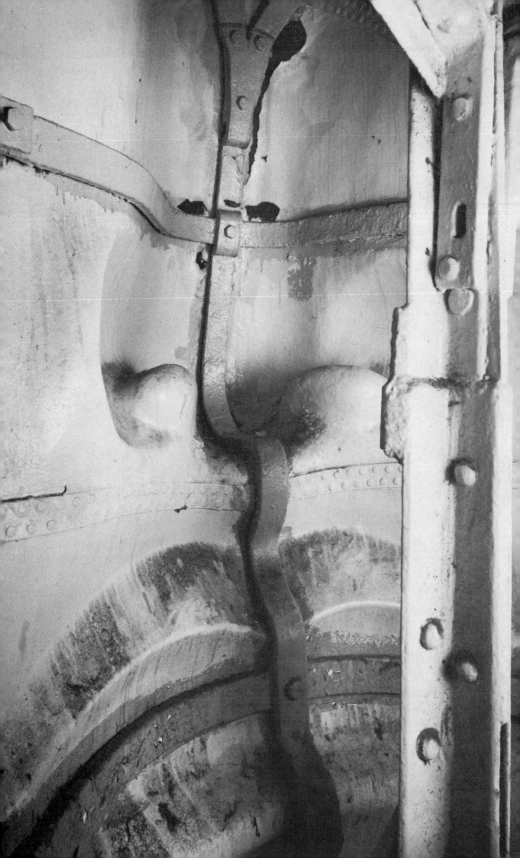

At this time the committee was not able to come up with the ideal method of removing the many layers of paint and tar without injuring Liberty's thin skin. Several aspects of Liberty's restoration would require inventiveness, experimentation, and even new technology. Paint removal from fragile copper sheeting was only one problem teams of scientists from different fields would have to explore and somehow solve.

The French-American Committee and the National Park Service had worked very hard on their study of Liberty and proposals for restoring her. Everyone agreed they had done an impressive and thorough job. Now all that remained was to find the millions of dollars necessary to restore her to her former strength and beauty.

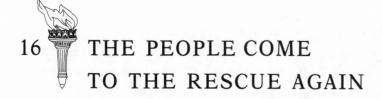

16 THE PEOPLE COME
TO THE RESCUE AGAIN

The well-publicized, thorough report of the French-American Committee brought the plight of the Statue of Liberty to the attention of the United States government and the American people. Certainly her repair had to take place without delay. There was no question about that.

One plan often leads to another. While they were talking about restoring Liberty, it occurred to many people who were involved that Ellis Island is an official part of the Statue of Liberty National Monument and the buildings there had been far more neglected than the lady on Liberty Island. After it ceased being an immigration station in 1954, the isolated island became easy prey for vandals, who stripped away plumbing, chandeliers, woodwork, and irreplaceable artifacts from the magnificent buildings that had originally been designed to impress newcomers to America. Without necessary upkeep, the marine environment created further damage. Seawalls crumbled into the harbor and docks collapsed. Finally the roofs began to cave in, allowing water to cause terrible structural damage. The grounds and pathways became overgrown with weeds.

Very little was done to improve Ellis Island after it became a part of the Statue of Liberty National Monument in 1965. The approaching birthday of the Statue of Liberty, however, provided an opportunity to do something about the shameful condition of the island where so many Americans had first set foot on a new land.

A very thorough study would have to be undertaken before anyone could say just what should be done with the ruins of the thirty-five buildings on Ellis Island. In the meantime, while there was general agreement that there was no point in restoring all of the buildings, there was a firm commitment to restoring the main immigration building by the statue's centennial. Full restoration of Ellis Island would have to await the island's own centennial in 1992.

There was also talk of encouraging private investors to open ethnic restaurants and craft shops in some of the old buildings so that visitors might taste the food of many nations or watch craftsmen from all over the world working on projects associated with their particular countries, such as Germans brewing beer or Armenians weaving rugs. It was hoped that the restoration of Ellis Island would remind Americans that they lived in a nation made strong by the contributions of people from many different countries.

All of these plans, of course, would cost a great deal of money. To do the job well, it was estimated that $230 million would be required. Building the statue one hundred years earlier had cost only $400,000. The money to be raised would be split up and spent in the following ways. Completely restoring the Statue of Liberty, preserving key buildings, and rebuilding the seawall on Ellis Island would cost $167 million. In order to maintain the Statue of Liberty and Ellis Island, $20 million was needed to set up a capital endowment for the two islands. The cost of conducting the fund-raising campaign would take $15 million. Another $28 million would be spent on educational programs and celebrations leading up to and including Liberty's birthday party.

Studying and planning for the renovations had taken almost two years. It was now time for the fund-raising and early repairs to begin. Again the United States government did not want to have any financial responsibility for the project. President Ronald Reagan had a philosophy that people ought to do things for themselves, and he pointed out that the original funds to build the statue had come from the people, including millions of pen-

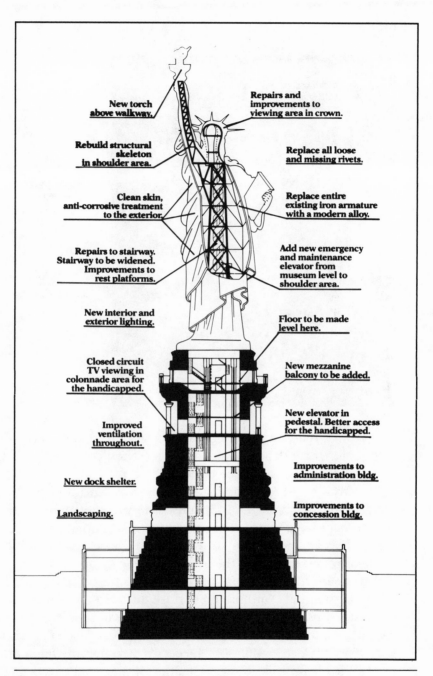

New torch above walkway.

Repairs and improvements to viewing area in crown.

Rebuild structural skeleton in shoulder area.

Replace all loose and missing rivets.

Clean skin, anti-corrosive treatment to the exterior.

Replace entire existing iron armature with a modern alloy.

Repairs to stairway. Stairway to be widened. Improvements to rest platforms.

Add new emergency and maintenance elevator from museum level to shoulder area.

New interior and exterior lighting.

Floor to be made level here.

Closed circuit TV viewing in colonnade area for the handicapped.

New mezzanine balcony to be added.

New elevator in pedestal. Better access for the handicapped.

Improved ventilation throughout.

Improvements to administration bldg.

New dock shelter.

Improvements to concession bldg.

Landscaping.

This diagram is the official National Park Service plan for the Statue of Liberty's restoration.

Lee Iacocca

nies from French and American school children. Liberty, he
said, belonged to the people, and they should be the ones to
take care of her in her time of need.

On May 18, 1982, President Reagan made an important announcement from the White House. He praised many of this
country's citizens who had been courageous enough to uproot
themselves and come to a strange land. He stressed the importance of preserving both the Statue of Liberty and Ellis Island
and announced the formation of the Statue of Liberty–Ellis
Island Centennial Commission to raise the $230 million needed.
It would consist of private citizens and be headed by Lee Iacocca, a highly successful businessman who was chairman of
the Chrysler Corporation. Mr. Iacocca's own parents had come
to America from Italy by way of Ellis Island.

Lee Iacocca invited twenty influential Americans to join him
on the fund-raising campaign commission. Among them were

Bob Hope and a former president of the United Auto Workers Union, Douglas Fraser.

To carry out the day-to-day activities necessary to raise money and educate the public, the commission set up an organization officially called the Statue of Liberty–Ellis Island Foundation, Inc. Office space on Park Avenue in New York City was rented that same month from which the foundation could carry on its campaign.

It began with a staff of eight people. As in Liberty's previous fund-raising drives, an attempt was first made to gather large donations. The official opening date of the campaign was July 4, 1984, and the closing date for collecting the $230 million would be October 28, 1986, Liberty's birthday.

Foundation members first thought they would start out by making fund-raising plans, but the statue's plight had been so well publicized that money began pouring in much earlier and in greater quantities than anyone associated with the campaign had ever dreamed possible. In the past, fund drives for Liberty had always been struggles, if not downright failures. This fund drive, at least in its beginning years, was different. The Statue of Liberty was now loved and revered by rich and poor, young and old. The foundation in New York in less than a year had to increase its staff to over a hundred employees, and regional offices were opened in various cities throughout the country.

As the national campaign got under way, Liberty's image began to appear frequently in magazines, in newspapers, and on television either to help a company sell its products or services or to publicize the renovation and centennial plans. Since the statue is a public figure, anyone is entitled to use her image in advertising whether or not money has been donated for the restoration. The only thing therefore that the foundation had to give their corporate sponsors was permission to use the official logo seal on their advertisements. Anyone seeing the head of Liberty with the words "Official Sponsor" printed above and the dates "1886–1986" below would know that the advertiser was indeed an official sponsor of the Statue of Liberty.

Since a great deal of respect and prestige was gained from

being recognized as a corporate sponsor, it was not long before giant corporations such as Chrysler, U.S. Tobacco, Coca-Cola, Eastman Kodak, American Airlines, and *U.S.A. Today* had signed multimillion dollar pledges to become corporate sponsors. Within a year after the foundation was set up, over $50,000,000 had already been donated by large corporations.

Many of these corporations contributed more than money, however. Materials for the restoration as well as services were donated. Allied Van Lines provided moving vans to take around to shopping centers all over the country exhibits about the statue and Ellis Island. Kodak made a fascinating offer to the public. For ten dollars, a contributor could send in his or her name and a family picture that Kodak promised to include in a computer program at Liberty or Ellis Island to be called the Kodak Family Album.

As the money began to come in, the Ellis Island architectural team completed their study of the immigration area. They talked over their ideas with foundation members, and definite plans were made for restoring the main immigration building. The building needed a new roof, the outside brick walls required extensive repair, and every door and window would have to be replaced. On the inside, walls would have to be taken down to restore the Great Hall, the Baggage Room, the Money Exchange, and the railroad area to their former grand size. One of the four stairways leading to the Great Hall also needed repair.

In addition to fixing up the old rooms, new features would be added. Two theaters would be constructed to show movies of the island's colorful history. A new auditorium was planned for concerts and performances by the best of music and drama groups from many different cultures.

There would be an immigration museum, which would be larger than the museum on Liberty Island and would contain more than immigration artifacts, such as old chairs and tables. There would be a library for immigration research, housing the old immigration records that researchers found were amazingly

The railroad ticket office on Ellis Island

complete. The museum planners also decided to record accounts by Ellis Island immigrants themselves for an oral history area.

Plans for using computers to recount the immigration story were very exciting. For a fee of something like five dollars, a visitor would be able to punch in his last name, and a computer would then probe its memory and list all the people with the same last name who had come through Ellis Island, complete with dates and ship names. There would also be a listing of immigrants who had similar last names but with slightly different spellings.

There would be yet another way to use the computer. A user could punch in a time period, say 1903 to 1908, along with the name of a village or town in the country from which his or her family emigrated. The computer would then present a list of all the people who emigrated to the United States from that particular village during those years. The money raised by these computer programs would go toward the maintenance of Liberty and Ellis islands.

Over the summer of 1983 a team of architects took careful measurements of the main building on Ellis Island. By the end of the summer they had enough information to begin making designs for the actual restoration.

At summer's end members of the Statue of Liberty–Ellis Island Foundation, pleased with how the corporate fund drive was going, decided to begin making plans for an official appeal to individuals. They did not want the money for Liberty's restoration to come mostly from large corporations. Liberty had always belonged to the people, and they wanted to make sure everybody would be given the opportunity to assist in her restoration.

It is hoped that the Great Hall on Ellis Island will be fully restored by the Statue of Liberty's one hundredth birthday in 1986.

To help them get in touch with people all over the country, the foundation hired the services of a direct-mail specialist who had been in charge of fund-raising for the Republican National Committee. In September 1983, a letter was prepared and mailed to almost half a million people. The response was overwhelming. The foundation heard from far more people than was anticipated, and the average donation was thirty dollars, which was much higher than is usually received from fund-raising letters.

The plans had been to try out different letters throughout much of 1984, but the September 1983 letter was so successful that the foundation decided to forget about further testing. They also decided not to wait for the official start of the fund drive on July 4, 1984. If the people wanted to give now, then they must be encouraged to do so. Accordingly, a letter appealing for funds was sent out to 28,000,000 people.

School children also began to respond before the official school campaign began. The statue had become a very familiar figure, almost a second mother and a friend. Children all over the country genuinely felt sorry for her and wanted to help her. In fact, they began sending in donations before there was even an official committee to receive them or to thank them for their gifts.

By the beginning of 1984, more than enough money had been raised to begin the work on the statue. On January 24, 1984, the first of four bargeloads of construction materials to be used for the scaffolding was taken to Liberty Island. Workers began erecting the 300-ton aluminum scaffold that would rise to the entire 151-foot-1-inch height of the statue and remain there until 1986.

The following month the *New York Daily News* announced it would be making an all-out effort to raise funds, comparing itself to *The World*, the newspaper of the "people," which one hundred years earlier had succeeded in raising the $102,000 needed to finish work on the pedestal. Someone commented that in 1984 that amount would barely pay for repairing the

In classrooms all around the country children act out the story of the Statue of Liberty in preparation for the centennial.

hem on Liberty's skirt. But in 1984 America was richer, and the country's population had increased substantially. The *Daily News*, as *The World* had done in the past, appealed to the American people by carrying on a widespread educational program in schools and creating interest by holding such things as photography and writing contests.

The promise of publishing the name of every donor had brought *The World* hundreds of donations. A similar promise was made by the *Daily News*, but the only way to list all the donors this time was in a computer printout.

The foundation staff in New York included a group called the Student Campaign Committee, headed by a former public school teacher named Sheila McCauley. The Student Campaign Committee did more than just encourage students to contribute money; it prepared a Student Campaign Manual containing information, suggested lesson plans, and ideas for fund-raising and mailed copies to schools from coast to coast. Major newspapers were also encouraged to print and pass out information and study guides for school use. Lee Iacocca himself wrote a moving letter to the students of the nation asking for their help and suggesting ways to raise money. Another formidable and time-consuming job of the Student Campaign Committee was to make sure all school groups were properly thanked for their fund-raising efforts.

On Friday, April 27, 1984, the freestanding scaffolding had finally reached the torch. From Manhattan, New Jersey, or from the harbor the statue appeared to be confined in a cage with thousands of horizontal and vertical bars. To celebrate the completion of the scaffolding, Lee Iacocca took a ceremonial ride up to the crown on the open scaffold elevator.

It had been hoped that the statue could remain open during the restoration, but when blasting with liquid nitrogen supplied by Union Carbide was chosen as the method to get rid of interior paint, it was decided to close the statue to climbing visitors. The temperature of the liquid nitrogen was 350° F below zero (or minus 212° C). The paint was literally being frozen off the walls. It was a noisy, dangerous process, and visitors simply could not be permitted.

Therefore, at closing time on May 29, 1984, the elevators and stairways at the Statue of Liberty were locked to all visitors

---

Visitors see Liberty with her completed scaffolding as they approach from the island walks.

and would remain closed until the statue was ready to open again on July 4, 1986. It would be the longest time the statue had ever been closed to the public. The island, however, and the American Museum of Immigration would remain open.

While work was beginning on the statue itself, the fund-raising drive gathered momentum. The foundation felt its corporate donation push had so far been enormously successful. Twelve giant corporations had given at least $5 million apiece, contributing $71 million toward the $230 million goal.

Mr. Iacocca began his own consumer drive by placing a beautiful picture of the Statue of Liberty surrounded by the rosy glow of sunset on the back cover of *Life* magazine's special issue on the Olympics. Over 1.2 million copies went out to newstands all over America. The Chrysler Corporation bought all the advertising for the entire issue.

Four television commercials were prepared for airing over the summer of 1984. The first had actress Louise Fletcher as the voice of Liberty pleading, "If you still believe in me, save me," while an aircraft carrying a camera circled the statue. The second had scores of school children singing "My Country 'Tis of Thee" at the base of the statue. A third was done by Charles Schultz featuring the Peanuts gang, and the fourth featured Mr. Iacocca on Liberty Island on the Fourth of July as the statue's torch was removed for replacement.

On the Fourth of July, the official starting date for the fund drive, Mr. Iacocca proudly announced at a ceremony at the statue that over $100 million had already been donated. The fact that the money was being raised so successfully was a tribute to the American people. Credit also had to be given to those in charge of the fund drive.

Of course, many other things, like the art of fund-raising had come a long way in a hundred years. Auguste Bartholdi had to raise most of the funds for France's gift to the United States almost singlehandedly. At one point when he was running out of funds, he had held a luncheon on a platform erected on the lap of the uncompleted statue. In the 1980s big fund-raising was

The Statue of Liberty's torch is removed as part of the July 4, 1984, celebration, and the fund drive for Liberty's restoration is officially under way.

a scientific business aided by computers, social scientists, and market-testing techniques. The restoration fund drive was highly successful in reaching the American people through personal letters and print and television commercials.

Mr. Iacocca was proud of the work of the foundation and grateful for the generosity of the American people as he and the other Fourth of July celebrants on Liberty Island turned their eyes upward to watch the construction crew getting ready to remove the 98-year-old torch. Some historians said the removal of the torch was the most dramatic alteration ever done to an American monument. Fred Harris, however, the construction worker who operated the hoist, said that lifting the one-and-a-half-ton torch was "a piece of cake, just another lift." Others, including Superintendent Moffitt, were quite nervous until they saw the torch safely on the ground.

For the rest of the day New Yorkers celebrated the Fourth in the usual ways. It was particularly evident that New York City is composed of people who have come from countries all over the world. In lower Manhattan celebrators at a street fair chose from refreshment stands offering shrimp tempura, burritos, and falafel. They stared with amusement as a Turkish belly dancer performed at an outdoor plaza.

In Brooklyn, a West German teenager, a member of her country's national judo team, who had never seen a hot dog before (and probably never wanted to see one again), wolfed down nine and a half hot dogs to win the annual Nathan's contest on Coney Island to see who could eat the most hot dogs in ten minutes' time.

As it got dark, millions of people ended the day by gathering to watch two spectacular fireworks displays bursting over the torchless figure of Liberty.

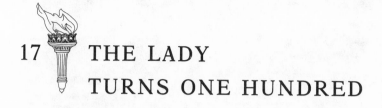

17 THE LADY
TURNS ONE HUNDRED

After the Fourth of July hoopla, it was business as usual on Liberty Island. Even though the Statue of Liberty was closed to the public, the hourly ferries continued to bring many visitors, who walked around the island, visited the museum, and watched the workmen, who looked like tiny insects high on the scaffolding. They got a good look at the battered torch resting on the ground awaiting the completion of the building that would house it while the new one was constructed.

Inside the statue, workmen, often with sweat running off their heavily muscled arms, continued blasting the old blue-green paint from the monument's skin with liquid nitrogen fired from guns. Even though the nitrogen was chilled to minus 350° Farenheit (minus 212° Celsius), temperatures were at least ten degrees hotter inside the statue than outside. In addition, the spray guns made a deafening echo inside the tube of Liberty's body, and the workers were surrounded by a blizzard of paint chips. On hot, summer days it was almost unbearable. To take a breather, workmen would step out on a balcony to cool off in a salt-scented sea breeze.

On nearby Ellis Island the summer of 1984 was spent cleaning out the old immigration building. The enormous amount of rubble collected over the years was carefully sorted. Important artifacts were picked out and saved for use in the museum or in the restored rooms.

The old torch waits outside for the new workshop to be built on Liberty Island.

A workman removes old paint from Liberty's skin with a blast of liquid nitrogen.

By the fall of 1984 work had been completed on the workshop at the base of the statue, and skilled artisans had begun to take measurements of the old torch in order to construct the new one. As the leaves fell and it got colder, the numbers of people visiting Liberty Island diminished. Still, for that time of year, there was a larger than usual number of visitors coming on the island ferries.

Ellis Island was closed to the public in September, and workers then arrived to tear down walls and begin the reconstruction work. Ellis Island would probably not reopen until the statue's centennial.

Children returning to school continued to learn about and discuss the Statue of Liberty and Ellis Island in their classrooms around the country. They kept on with their fund-raising and frequently sent letters along with their checks. Members of the Student Campaign Committee were often moved to laughter or tears by the children's letters. Mr. Pulitzer had shared the letters he received over a hundred years earlier by printing them in *The World*, but it was far more difficult to share the children's letters with the country at large in the current fund drive because sensational news tended to get priority.

One story in particular had everybody at the foundation offices chuckling. In California a number of school groups raised money by selling foot-long chocolate candy bars in the shape of the statue. The Nestlé Company provided the candy bars to be used for the children's fund-raising activities. A second-grader took orders from twenty family members and friends. When he picked up his order at school, he discovered that the statue candy bars had come complete with torches. Since the Statue of Liberty now had no torch, he solved the problem by carefully biting off and eating all twenty of his chocolate torches before delivering the candy bars to his customers.

A school class from Alaska sent a check for $111.00. One of the children sent a letter along saying, "I certainly hope this is enough to clean a fingernail."

As the year came to an end, it was decided to display the old torch on a float in the annual Tournament of Roses Parade held

Two fourth-graders raised money by buying replicas of the Statue of Liberty in Nestlé chocolate and are now enjoying their purchases.

in Pasadena, California, on New Year's Day. The craftsmen were reluctant to lose their model, but everyone agreed it was a good idea. American Airlines offered to fly the torch out to California, but at the last minute the company was unable to provide the transportation it had promised. The Flying Tigers, a freight line staffed mostly by ex-World War II pilots, came to the rescue. The torch was carefully packed in a box with transparent sides for the trip.

Corporations continued to donate money, materials, and interesting services. A company called Gold Leaf from Tallahassee, Florida, paid the National Park Service an estimated $12 million for the exclusive rights to all the materials removed from Liberty and Ellis islands during the renovation. They planned to sell chips of material removed from the statue as souvenirs and to melt down some of the metal to make commemorative pieces such as desk ornaments and key chains. They were also willing to make arrangements to sell some of the materials to other interested buyers.

By the beginning of 1985 school children had given $2 million. Children from the Bauder Elementary School in Seminole, Florida, had the honor at that point of having given more money than any other school in the nation. Led by their enthusiastic principal, Pat Goodwin, the 850 children from varied ethnic backgrounds spent much of the 1983–84 school year studying the statue and Ellis Island in many of their classes. On a beautiful spring day in May, near the close of the school year, the children invited all the other schools in the area to attend a giant field day. Part of the day's activities was a Walk for Liberty. They raised $12,000, and their principal, a teacher, and a few children were flown to New York to appear on the "Good Morning America" television show to share their impressive fund-raising efforts with the nation.

Even the federal government, which had always managed to avoid fund-raising activities for the statue, seemed on the verge of becoming part of the growing popular movement to save the monuments in New York harbor. On January 3, 1985, the House

The Statue of Liberty's old torch has an honored place in the January 1, 1985, Tournament of Roses Parade.

of Representatives began considering legislation that would create three new coins to commemorate the centennial. The most expensive coin would be a five-dollar gold piece, which would carry a picture of the statue on it. The second coin would be a silver dollar and would be imprinted with a picture of Ellis Island. The third coin would be a half dollar and would feature some kind of tribute to immigrants and the contributions they have made to the United States. Representative Frank Annunzio, the Illinois Democrat who suggested the idea, estimated that up to $137.5 million could be raised from the new coins, which would be sold at a surcharge to the public. That would be more than half of the $230 million goal!

Some years ago, because copper was so expensive, it had been suggested that a two-cent piece with a picture of the Statue of Liberty on it should replace the penny. For some reason that idea was rejected, and the one-cent piece was saved. This time, however, members of Congress seemed to think the three coins featuring the Statue of Liberty and Ellis Island stood a good chance of being issued because raising money for the restoration was such a popular cause.

By the beginning of 1985 the foundation staff turned its attention to making plans for the centennial celebration. Though they knew they would probably have to make a number of alterations before everything was finalized, they hoped to have a proposed schedule of events ready to present to the public by the spring of 1985.

Of this much they were sure. The celebration of Liberty's birthday would begin on July 4, 1986, and continue throughout the country all summer long. The Fourth of July would be a festive day, again featuring a parade of the tall ships and culminating in the attaching of Liberty's new torch. On that day the statue would once again be open to the public. The Fourth of July would end, of course, with nationwide fireworks, the largest display of all showering over New York harbor and Liberty.

The summer of celebration would end with a solemn ceremony of rededication on October 28, 1986, the statue's real one hundredth birthday. It was hoped that the presidents of the United States and France would attend.

One of the events planned was the result of an exciting discovery made in Paris by a lady named Nancy Sureck, the director of cultural and special events for the Statue of Liberty–Ellis Island Foundation. After doing a lot of poking around in French museums and libraries, Ms. Sureck found the original manuscript of the cantata called "Liberty Enlightening the World" composed by Charles Gounod and performed with a large male choir and a full orchestra at the Paris Opera on April 25, 1876, as a fund-raising event. The piece was never performed again.

In late February 1985, the handwritten manuscript was carefully and ceremoniously brought to the United States by François de Laboulaye, the French Ambassador to the United States from 1977 to 1982 and a descendent of Édouard de Laboulaye, and put on display at the Pierpont Morgan Library in New York City. It was hoped that the piece could be revived for Liberty's centennial celebration, but unfortunately very few musical groups in the country could afford the lavish production written by Gounod. A conductor in New York City named Hugh Ross was given the job of simplifying the score so the work could be performed by a mixed choir accompanied by a piano, an organ, or a small brass ensemble. The Statue of Liberty–Ellis Island Foundation paid to have the newly arranged score printed up for use by choral societies and school choruses all over the country. The French lyrics were translated into English and in some cases changed to fit the occasion. The opening words became, "I have triumphed! I am 100 years old! My name is Liberty!"

At the statue work was going along on schedule. The new torch was being constructed at one end of the workshop at the base of Liberty. At the other end metal workers were painstakingly duplicating the rusted, curvy old ribs in stainless steel. However, it became necessary to close the whole island to the public in June 1985, and it would not reopen until July 4, 1986.

Inside the statue, the paint had all been frozen off the interior skin by liquid nitrogen. Workmen had found, however, that liquid nitrogen did not have a strong enough effect on the many layers of paint on Liberty's central pylon and secondary framework. After carefully covering Liberty's exposed fragile interior skin with tarps, they began to attack the layers of paint on the iron skeletal system by sandblasting. Most of the flying paint chips were immediately sucked up by a vacuum cleaner hose

A new rib being constructed in the spacious workshop on Liberty Island.

that surrounded the blasting tube, but there were still so many bits of lead in the air that workers had to wear spacesuits equipped with a pure air supply. Breathing the air in the statue might have led to lead poisoning. For a while the cramped interior of Liberty resembled a science-fiction movie.

Another problem that had to be solved by the renovators was how to carry out the committee's request that 2 percent of the copper skin of Liberty be replaced with artificially aged new plates. The technology to achieve this feat had yet to be invented. A team of metal scientists had to be asked to help.

The worst places, which in some cases were corroded all the

At first glance removing layers of tar and paint looked like an impossible task. Note the rivet holes where the saddles have pulled loose.

way through, were where water had collected—in the folds of Liberty's gown and in her curls—and there was also a bad spot on her upper lip. In all four hundred square feet of copper needed to be replaced.

Nothing the scientists tried seemed to work. They spent six months climbing the scaffolding to experiment with different ways of applying copper patches so they wouldn't look like patches. They could not match the colors, and the various acid solutions with which they tried to age the new copper seemed likely to weaken the metal too much. Finally, when they had almost given up, one member of the team, John Franey, a corrosion specialist for AT&T's Bell Laboratories, was driving past his firm's buildings in Murray Hill, New Jersey, one day on his way to work. He just happened to notice workmen removing an old copper roof from the auditorium. Suddenly he knew the problem was solved but not in the way he and his colleagues had anticipated.

On April 4, 1985, John Franey proudly climbed aboard a boat that delivered to Liberty Island fifteen crates of copper strips the perfect shade of green to match the statue. In return for the copper roofing, Bell Laboratories asked for Liberty's corroded copper sections so they could study what happens to copper as it corrodes naturally under a variety of weather conditions.

Liberty also benefited by recent discoveries made by scientists trying to solve problems that had nothing to do with the lady on Liberty Island. For years sailors have had to spend long hours chipping rust from corroded decks. When the Naval Research Laboratory came up with a paste for removing rust from irregular or difficult-to-reach surfaces aboard Navy ships, it was decided the same material could be applied to Liberty's rusty

---

Liberty's head has suffered from the weather more than most other parts of her body. The sets of three holes are from saddles that have popped their rivets or may have never been filled at all. Weak spots in her upper lip and curls need to be replaced with matching aged copper sheets.

spots. Depending on the thickness of the rust, the paste was left on the statue for several days. After that it was easily peeled off, leaving behind a clean surface totally free of rust.

There have indeed been many ways of solving problems for Liberty from the time that Auguste Bartholdi conceived the project more than a century ago to the present. It was his hope that the statue would last as long as the pyramids. Looking back, one would have to agree the first one hundred years for Lady Liberty have not been easy. She arrived as a stranger in a country where most people either ignored her or wished she would go away. At first she towered over the New York skyline, but she was soon dwarfed by tall buildings. On her small island she was neglected and often abused. It took a wave of immigrants to give her recognition as a Mother of Exiles and two terrible world wars to make her mother of a nation and a true American.

As she approaches her hundredth birthday, she is being well taken care of and is cherished not only by Americans but also by people everywhere as a symbol of liberty and freedom. It is said that the centennial restoration will enable the Statue of Liberty to withstand conditions in New York harbor for the next one thousand years. That's a pretty impressive prediction, but most of us would like to think she will be there forever.

Everyone hopes that children—and grownups, too, of course—will be able to continue visiting the Statue of Liberty for many centuries to come.

LIBERTY'S MEASUREMENTS

THE STATUE

Height (base to torch)	151 feet 1 inch
Height (foundation to torch)	305 feet 1 inch
Height of torch	21 feet
Head from chin to cranium	17 feet 3 inches
Distance across an eye	2 feet 6 inches
Length of nose	4 feet 6 inches
Width of mouth	3 feet
Length of right arm	42 feet
Greatest thickness of right arm	12 feet
Length of hand	16 feet 5 inches
Length of index finger	8 feet
Circumference of finger (at second joint)	3 feet 6 inches
Size of fingernail	13 × 10 inches
Length of tablet	23 feet 7 inches
Width of tablet	13 feet 7 inches
Thickness of tablet	2 feet
Thickness of copper sheathing (varies because of hammer forming)	⅛ to 3/32 inch

Weight of copper used	100 tons
Weight of iron used	125 tons
Total weight of statue	225 tons

THE PEDESTAL

Height	89 feet
Width of one side at base	65 feet
Width of one side at top	43 feet
Heights of Grecian columns above base	72 feet 8 inches

THE FOUNDATION

Height	53 feet
Width of one side at bottom	91 feet
Width of one side at top	65 feet

MISCELLANEOUS FACTS

Steps in statue (base to crown)	171 steps
Steps in pedestal	167 steps
Rungs in ladder from beginning of right arm to torch	54 rungs
Windows in crown	25 windows
Rays in diadem	7 rays
Inscription on tablet in left hand	July 4, 1776 (in Roman numerals)
Initial cost to build	$400,000 for the statue $270,000 for the pedestal
Number of persons who could fit comfortably into head area	40 people
Number of persons who could fit comfortably on torch balcony	12 people

CHRONOLOGY
OF IMPORTANT EVENTS

1865 The idea for the statue is born at Édouard de Laboulaye's dinner party.

1871 Auguste Bartholdi makes his first trip to America.

1875 The French-American Union is formed, and work on Liberty begins.

1876 Bartholdi makes his second trip to the United States, Liberty's arm is displayed in Philadelphia, and Auguste Bartholdi marries Jeanne-Emilie Baheux de Puysieux.

1877 President Grant signs a resolution accepting the gift of Liberty Enlightening the World to be used as a beacon. The American Committee of the French-American Union is established to raise funds for the pedestal and foundation.

1878 Liberty's head is displayed at the Paris Universal Exhibition.

1879 Gustave Eiffel is asked to design Liberty's interior framework and Richard Morris Hunt the pedestal; General Charles P. Stone is chosen as the engineer in charge of the pedestal and foundation construction.

1883 "The New Colossus," a poem written by Emma Lazarus, is published in *The World* poetry contest.

1884 The statue is completed in Paris and presented to the United States in a ceremony that takes place in France.

1885 Liberty is disassembled, packed in crates, and shipped to the United States. Enough money is raised during Joseph Pulitzer's newspaper campaign to complete the pedestal.

1886 The statue is dedicated and officially begins her first one hundred years in America.

1892 A federal immigration station opens at Ellis Island.

1901 Thanks to President Theodore Roosevelt, necessary reforms take place on Ellis Island.

1902 The Lighthouse Board turns over to the War Department the responsibility for Liberty.

1903 Emma Lazarus's poem "The New Colossus" is inscribed on a bronze tablet and placed within Liberty's pedestal.

1916 The Black Tom munitions explosion takes place, and Liberty receives a new lighting plant. The torch is remodeled by sculptor Gutzon Borglum.

1924 By a proclamation of President Coolidge, the Statue of Liberty becomes a National Monument.

1925 William A. Simpson becomes the first superintendent in charge of the Liberty Monument.

1931 A new floodlighting system is installed in Liberty.

1933 Responsibility for the Liberty Monument moves from the War Department to the Department of the Interior.

1936 Liberty celebrates her fiftieth birthday.

1937 The United States Army leaves Bedloe's Island, and the entire island is turned over to the National Park Service. Extensive repairs begin with labor and funds provided by federal public works projects.

1941 When Pearl Harbor is bombed and the United States enters World War II, the lights are turned off at the Statue of Liberty.

1945 World War II ends, and the statue lights go on again.

1954 The immigration station at Ellis Island closes.

1960 Bedloe's Island is renamed Liberty Island.

1965 President Johnson announces that Ellis Island has become part of the Statue of Liberty National Monument.

1972 The American Museum of Immigration opens in Liberty's pedestal.

1976 Liberty is featured in the country's Bicentennial celebration.

1980 Liberty is scaled by two protesters, and an investigation leads to the formation of the French-American Committee for Restoration of the Statue of Liberty.

1982 The Statue of Liberty–Ellis Island Centennial Commission is formed to run a huge fund-raising drive for the restoration of the Statue of Liberty and Ellis Island.

1984 The fund-raising drive officially begins, and the torch is removed.

1986 Lady Liberty celebrates her hundredth birthday.

ACKNOWLEDGMENTS

Several members of the National Park Service were very helpful in the preparation of this book. I would like to thank in particular librarian Won Kim and museum technician Lonnie McQuire, both National Park Service employees on Liberty Island, for their invaluable assistance in finding useful government reports, giving information, and providing photographs. Park ranger Kathy Kusch's inspired guided tour of Ellis Island was the source of much of the information in the chapter on Ellis Island. It will be a shame if she is replaced by talking cassettes and computers as is being threatened.

I wish also to thank a number of enthusiastic, informed people who work at the Statue of Liberty–Ellis Island Foundation including F. Ross Holland, Jr., Edward W. Dooley, Pepper Birchard, and Sheila McCauley, who talked to me at length about restoration, fund-raising, and centennial plans.

In addition, the publisher and I are grateful for the time and effort contributed by Marlene Bergstrom and Eric Delony of Robert J. Kapsch's HABS/HAER office in Washington, D.C., in collecting photographs for the book.

Finally, I would like to thank Trinity School in New York City, where I am the elementary school librarian, for its support and understanding; and my husband, Robert Hipkens, and my daughter Sarah, who encouraged me to neglect them while I worked on this book.

BIBLIOGRAPHY

Arena, Salvatore. "N.Y. Sings Torch Song." *New York Daily News*, July 5, 1984, Sec. III, p. 3.

Barbanel, Josh. "Statue of Liberty Damaged by Two Protesters." *The New York Times*, May 11, 1980, Sec. I, p. 1.

Bigart, Homer. "4 Held in Plot to Blast Statue of Liberty, Liberty Bell and Washington Monument." *The New York Times*, February 17, 1965, Sec. I, p. 1.

"Beauty Treatment for Miss Liberty." *Literary Digest*, Vol. III (December 1931), p. 25.

Bell, James B., and Richard I. Abrams. *In Search of Liberty: The Story of the Statue of Liberty and Ellis Island*. Garden City, N.Y.: Doubleday and Company, 1984.

"Body of Iron, Soul of Fire." Film made by the American Express Company for the National Park Service, 1972.

Brock, H. I. "Liberty's New Dress." *New York Times Magazine*, July 4, 1948, Sec. I, p. 12.

Centennial for Liberty, 1886–1986. The Statue of Liberty–Ellis Island Foundation, Inc., 1983.

Clines, Francis. "About New York: At Home With Miss Liberty." *The New York Times*, October 6, 1977, Sec. II, p. 1.

Cook, Joan. "Home for This Select Group Is Where the Statue of Liberty Is." *The New York Times*, June 15, 1968, Sec. I, p. 28.

"Cover Lady of the Harbor." *New York Daily News*, April 28, 1984, p. 10.

Diamond, Stuart. "Technology: Statue's Repair Aids Research." *The New York Times*, February 14, 1985, Sec. IV, p. 2.

Dougherty, Philip. "Advertising: The Statue of Liberty Campaign." *The New York Times*, June 13, 1984, Sec. IV, p. 16.

Dowd, Maureen. "New Yorkers Celebrate a Dandy Fourth of July." *The New York Times*, July 5, 1984, Sec. II, p. 3.

Edelson, Edward. "A Monumental Job." *New York Sunday News Magazine*, February 19, 1984, pp. 10–12.

"Ellis Island Cast in a Historic Roll; To Be a Part of Liberty Island Project, Udall Says." *The New York Times*, January 7, 1965, Sec. I, p. 33.

"Ellis Island Commission." *The New York Times*, June 22, 1982, Sec. I, p. 18.

English, Bella. "Like 208 Candles!" *New York Daily News*, July 5, 1984, Sec. III, p. 5.

"Footbridge to Liberty Island Is Proposed by Jerseyan." *The New York Times*, October 7, 1962, Sec. I, p. 9.

Gentile, Don. "80G Slap to Miss Liberty." *New York Daily News*, May 11, 1980, pp. 3 and 52.

"Good News for Sailors." *The New York Times*, April 23, 1985, Sec. III, p.3.

"Group Holds Protest in Statue of Liberty Crown." *The New York Times*, February 16, 1977, Sec. II, p. 3.

Hamill, Pete. "Mother of Exiles." *New York Sunday News Magazine*, February 19, 1984, pp. 5–9 and 14–17.

Handlin, Oscar, and the editors of the *Newsweek* Book Division. *Statue of Liberty*. New York: Newsweek, 1971.

Hanrahan, Thomas. "Liberty Climbox: Nab 2, 80G Damage." *New York Daily News*, May 12, 1980, p. 3.

Heidish, Marcy. "The Grande Dame of the Harbor." *Geo*, Vol. 6 (July 1, 1984), pp. 36–45.

"Hello, AT&T? Could You Give the Statue of Liberty a Perm?" *The New York Times*, April 4, 1985, Sec. IV, p. 7.

Hirschfeld, Neal. "Isle of Tears." *New York Sunday News Magazine*, February 19, 1984, pp. 19–23.

"Hudson Legislator Asks Swivel for Miss Liberty." *The New York Times*, April 29, 1971, Sec. I, p. 45.

Hugins, Walter. *Statue of Liberty National Monument: Its Origin, Development and Administration*. U.S. National Park Service, 1958.

"Iacocca Outlines Ellis Island Plans." *The New York Times*, June 21, 1982, Sec. II, p. 3.

"Iacocca to Head Drive to Restore Landmarks." *The New York Times*, May 19, 1982, Sec. III, p. 20.

"Inspectors Find Statue Is Corroded." *The New York Times*, May 19, 1980, Sec. II, p. 1.

"Jersey City Chamber 'Conquers' Liberty Island." *The New York Times*, May 24, 1966, Sec. I, p. 49.

Kraske, Robert. *The Statue of Liberty Comes to America*. Champaign, Illinois: Garrard Press, 1972.

"Lady in a Cage." *Discover*, July 1984, pp. 18–25.

"Learning About Lady Liberty." *Instructor*, Vol. XCIII, No. 6 (February 1984), pp. 52–57.

"Liberty Enlightening the World." *Scientific American*, Vol. 52 (June 1885), pp. 375–376.

Liberty Enlightening the World, A Centennial Celebration, 1886–1986. Elementary School Curriculum Guide, prepared by the N.Y.C. Board of Education with the support of the *New York Daily News*, 1984.

McFadden, Robert D. "Iranians in Protest at Liberty Statue." *The New York Times*, November 5, 1979, Sec. I, p. 11.

Mercer, Charles. *Statue of Liberty*. New York: G. P. Putnam's Sons, 1979.

Miller, Natalie. *The Story of the Statue of Liberty*. Cornerstones of Freedom Series. Chicago: Children's Press, 1965.

"Miss Liberty Shines Through Blackout." *The New York Times*, November 10, 1965, Sec. I, p. 1.

Moritz, Owen. "Lady Dons Robe." *New York Daily News*, January 24, 1984, p. 3.

Nash, Margo. *Statue of Liberty: Keeper of Dreams*. Glendale, N.Y.: Berry Enterprises, 1983.

Nason, Thelma. *Our Statue of Liberty*. Chicago: Follett Publishing Company, 1969.

"1 Held, 1 Released in Climb of Statue." *The New York Times*, May 13, 1980, Sec. II, p. 4.

Reiter, Ed. "Three Coins Proposed for the Statue of Liberty." *The New York Times*, January 20, 1985, Sec. VIII, p. 33.

Robertson, Nan. "U.S. Premiere for Hymn to Statue of Liberty." *The New York Times*, February 28, 1985, Sec. III, p. 17.

Rogers, Frances. *Big Miss Liberty*. New York: Frederick A. Stokes Company, 1938.

"Role Symbolized for Miss Liberty. Museum of Immigration Is Dedicated on Island." *The New York Times*, October 29, 1962, Sec. I, p. 6.

Rush, George. "Taking Care of Miss Liberty." *Esquire*, July 1982, pp. 72–74.

Russell, John. "How Miss Liberty Was Born." *Smithsonian*, Vol. 15 (July 1984), pp. 46–55.

"Saving the Queen." *Newsweek*, August 1, 1983, p. 33.

"Scaffolding Ordered for Survey of Statue." *The New York Times*, May 14, 1980, Sec. II, p. 3.

Schumach, Murray. "A Fireworks Shelling of Harbor Due July 4." *The New York Times*, June 29, 1976, Sec. I, p. 21.

————. "Ranger Ends Idyll with Famed Lady." *The New York Times*, December 19, 1969, Sec. I, p. 57.

Simon, Kate. "Saluting the Statue of Liberty." *Travel and Leisure*, Vol. 14, No. 7 (July 1984), pp. 78–88.

Statue of Liberty: Architectural and Engineering Report. Prepared for the French-American Committee for Restoration of the Statue of Liberty, Inc., July 14, 1983.

"The Statue of Liberty Nearing Completion." *Scientific American*, Vol. 65 (August 14, 1886), p. 100.

"The Statue of Liberty, New York." *Scientific American*, Vol. 65 (November 20, 1886), p. 320.

"Statue of Liberty Occupied by Anti-Nixon Protesters." *The New York Times*, April 20, 1974, Sec. I, p. 35.

"Statue of Liberty Shut for Facelift." *The New York Times*, May 30, 1984, Sec. II, p. 4.

Stein, Conrad. *The Story of Ellis Island.* Cornerstones of Freedom Series. Chicago: Children's Press, 1979.

"They Rally 'Round the Torch." *New York Daily News*, May 27, 1984, pp. 72–73.

This Fabulous Century, Sixty Years of American Life. Six volumes. New York: Time-Life Books, 1969.

Trachtenberg, Marvin. *The Statue of Liberty.* New York: Penguin, 1977.

"2 Statue Climbers Charged With Trespass and Damage." *The New York Times*, May 12, 1980, Sec. II, p. 3.

"Udall Bars a Causeway to Statue of Liberty." *The New York Times*, July 25, 1963, Sec. I, p. 12.

"Warships of 22 Nations Arrive for Bicentennial." *The New York Times*, July 4, 1976, Sec. I, p. 1.

INDEX

Numbers in italics refer to illustrations.

Allied Van Lines, 158
American Airlines, 158, 174
American Committee of the
    French-American Union, 33
American Museum of Immigration,
    8, 9, 114, 117, 119, 121, 128
Armature
  concept of, 40–42
  problems with, 97, *145*, 146, 148,
    151
  restoration of, 10, 97, *98*, 148,
    149, 150, *178*
Army, U.S., *62*, 63, 85, 88, *93*, 94,
    95–97

Baheux de Puysieux, Jeanne-
    Emilie, 55
  meets Bartholdi, 20
  poses for statue, 26
  marriage to Bartholdi, 33
Bartholdi, Frédéric Auguste
  background information on, 14,
    15
  Egyptian statue plans, 16
  first visit to America, 16–22
  early sketches of the statue, *17*,
    18
  models for the statue, *24*, 25, 26
  second trip to America, 30, 33

marriage, 33
third trip to America, 50
at dedication ceremony, 54–55,
    56, 57
1890 interview, 63
death of, 79
Bartholdi, Madame, *27*, 54
  relationship with son, 18, 33
  posing for statue, 26
Bauder Elementary School, 174
Bedloe's (Liberty) Island, 18, 38,
    59–61, *60*, *62*, 85, *87*, 93,
    93, 94, 95, 100, *116*
  See also Living on Bedloe's (Lib-
    erty) Island
Bedloo, Issack, 59
Bicentennial celebration, U.S.,
    128–131, *130*
Black Tom explosion, 81
Borglum, Gutzon, 82, 146, *147*

Camp, Oswald E., 95, 101
Castle Garden, 66
Centennial celebration, 176–177,
    182
Centennial International Exhibi-
    tion in Philadelphia, 30,
    31, *32*

Ceremonies held at statue
  dedication ceremony, 52, 54–55,
    56, 57
  lighting ceremony (1916), 82,
    84
  lighting ceremony (1931), 90
  fiftieth anniversary, 95, 96
  Ellis Island becomes part of
    Statue of Liberty National
    Monument, 121, 122
  U.S. Bicentennial celebration,
    128–129, 130, 131
  statue's centennial celebration,
    176–177
Chain. See Shackle chain
Children, involvement in raising
    funds, 37, 48, 162, 163, 164,
    172, 173, 174
Chrysler Corporation, 156, 158, 166
Citizens Committee, 63, 77, 78, 79
Cleveland, President Grover, 52, 57
Coca-Cola, 158
Coins, proposed creation of to com-
    memorate centennial, 174–
    176
Construction of the statue
  in Paris, 26–29, 28, 29, 34,
    40–42, 41, 43, 44
  disassembling for shipment to
    the U.S., 48–50
  on Bedloe's Island, 50, 51
Coolidge, President Calvin, 85
Copper skin. See Skin, copper
Cost
  of the pedestal, 33, 45
  of the statue, 25, 34
  of 1907 repairs, 80
  of 1937–1938 repairs, 100
  of improvements to the island
    (1937–1938), 101
  of cleaning the statue and the is-
    land (1947), 110
  of completing the master plan
    (1950s), 113
  of erecting scaffolding, 140
  of centennial renovation, 154

Crawford, Pingree, 126
Crouse Hines, 129

Damage (man-made) to statue
  mistakes made during erection
    in New York harbor, 52
  Black Tom explosion, 81
  graffiti, 110, 111
  industrial grime, 88
  holes made for lighting torch, 54,
    82, 88, 89
  carbon dioxide, 143
  overpainting, 143
Damage, water, 145–148
Dedication ceremony, 52, 54–57, 56
Drummond, Edwin, 136–140, 139

Eastman Kodak, 158
Eiffel, Gustave
  background information on, 36–
    37, 39
  plan for interior framework, 37.
    40–42, 148
  only mistake, 42, 145
Ellis Island
  defense use of, 61
  as an immigration center, 5, 67,
    70–76, 71, 72, 76, 159
  immigration reforms, 78–79
  as a detention center, 107
  closing of immigration center,
    116–117
  becomes part of the Statue of
    Liberty National Monu-
    ment, 4, 121, 122
  restoration of, 153–154, 158–160,
    161, 169, 172
Evarts, William, 33, 52, 55, 57

Ferry service, 2, 3, 101, 114
Fiftieth anniversary, 94–95, 96

Financing the statue. *See* Fund-
    raising activities
Flying Tigers, 174
Fort Clinton, 66
Fort Wood, 38, 61, 77, 97
Foundation of statue, 38–40, 42
Franco-Prussian War, 16
Franey, John, 180
Fraser, Douglas, 157
French-American Committee for
    Restoration of the Statue
    of Liberty, 141, 142, 152,
    153
French-American Union, 23–25
Fund-raising activities
    first campaign in France, 25
    Bartholdi's efforts in U.S., 30, 33
    by displaying head at the Paris
        Universal Exhibition, 34,
        35
    French national lottery, 37
    for the pedestal in U.S., 45–49,
        50
    for repairs in 1916, 80, 82
    centennial restoration campaign,
        157-158, 160–162, 164,
        166–168, 172, *173*, 174,
        175, 176–177
    See also Children, involvement in
        raising funds

Gage, Secretary of the Treasury,
    78
Gaget, Gauthier and Company, 25,
    28, *29*, *31*, 34
Galvanic action in statue, 42, 58–
    59, 145
Gounod, Charles, 25, 177
Gold Leaf, 174
Graffiti on statue, 110, *111*
Grandjean, Philippe, 141
Grant, President Ulysses S., 20, 33,
    34, 62
Great Depression, 91, *92*

Hope, Bob, 157
Hunt, Richard Morris, *21*
    meets Bartholdi, 20
    chosen as architect for the pedes-
        tal, 37–38

Iacocca, Lee, 156, *156*, 164, 166,
    168
Immigration
    early history of, 64–66
    legislation following World War
        II, 112
    legislation in 1965, 121
    See also Ellis Island
Interior, Department of the, 92, 94,
    95
Interior environment of the statue,
    143
Interior framework
    Viollet-le-Duc plan, 30, 40
    Gustave Eiffel plan, 37, 40–42,
        41, 43
    problems with, 52
Isère, *49*, 50

Johnson, Philip, 121–123
Johnson, President Lyndon B., 121,
    122

Kennedy, Archibald, 59–60

Laboulaye, Édouard de
    background information on, 13,
        14, *15*
    dinner party at which the idea
        for the Statue of Liberty
        was born, 13, 14
    introduces statue plan to the
        French people, 23
LaFarge, John, 20, 33
LaFarge, Margaret, 33

Lafayette, Marquis de, statue of,
    23, 30
Landscaping around the statue and
    on the island, 61–62, 63,
    66, 97, 100, 101, 113
Lazarus, Emma, 46–48, 47, 76, 79,
    112
Lend-Lease plan, 103–104
Lesseps, Ferdinand D., 54
Liberty Enlightening the World,
    22, 30, 48
Liberty Island, 5–8, 118. See also
    Bedloe's (Liberty) Island
Liberty loan drives, 83, 84
Lighthouse Board, 62, 63, 77, 78
Lighthouse, Liberty as a, 34, 52–
    54, 62–63
Lighting of the statue
    electrifying torch, 52–54
    blacking out of the statue, 78,
        104
    major renovations, 82, 88–90, 89,
        106–107, 129, 150
    during 1965 blackout, 123
    See also Torch
Living on Bedloe's (Liberty) Island,
    59, 101–102, 104–105, 113–
    114, 124–126, 131, 132

Macy's Department Store, 129
McCauley, Sheila, 164
McManus, Edward, 140, 141
Marshall, Charles S., 107, 110
Master plan for the island, 97,
    100–101, 113–114
Moffitt, Dave, 131–132, 134, 135,
    135, 136–140
Mother of Exiles, 48, 76, 112

Napoleon III, 14, 16
National Monument
    statue designated as, 86
    Ellis Island becomes a part of,
        121

National Park Service, 92, 93, 94,
    97, 100, 101, 102, 114, 140,
    141, 142, 152, 174
Nestlé Company, 172
"New Colossus, The," 46–47, 79.
    See also Lazarus, Emma
New Jersey's interest in the statue
    and the island, 60–61, 118–
    119, 123–124, 127
New York Daily News, 162–164

Palmer, George A., 94–95, 101, 105
Paris Universal Exhibition, 34, 35
Patina, 79–80, 142
Pedestal of the statue, 37, 38, 50,
    90, 143
Pierpont Morgan Library, 177
Presentation of the statue to the
    United States, 42
Protests held at the statue, 86–88,
    120–121, 122–124, 127–128,
    131–132, 133, 134–135, 140
Pulitzer, Joseph, 46, 47, 48, 66–67,
    172

Reagan, President Ronald, 154–156
Repairs and renovations
    1907 repairs, 80
    Borglum torch, 82
    1931 lighting improvements, 88–
        90, 89
    public works renovations, 93, 97,
        98, 99, 100–102
    wire mesh around stairway, 110,
        111, 112
    completing master plan, 113–114
    centennial renovation, 140, 142–
        145, 148–152, 151, 155,
        164, 165, 168, 169, 170,
        171, 172, 177–182, 178,
        179, 181
Ribs. See Armature

Roosevelt, President Franklin D.,
    91–92, 95, *96*, 97, 103–104,
    106
Roosevelt, President Theodore,
    78
Ross, Hugh, 177
Rutherford, Steven, 136, 138

Shackle chain, 9, 25
Simpson, William A., 86–90
Skin, copper
    reason for using, 25–26
    construction of, 29, *29*
    attachment to armature, 40–42,
        43
    problems with, 50–52, *54*, 79–80,
        88, 142–143
    repair of, *171*, 178–180, *179*, *181*
Spikes in crown, 25, 97, *99*
Staircase, spiral, from base to
    crown, 143–144, *144*
Statue of Liberty–Ellis Island Cen-
    tennial Commission, 156–
    157
Statue of Liberty–Ellis Island
    Foundation, Inc., 157, 177
Stone, Charles P., 38, *39*, 40, 50
Student Campaign Committee,
    164, 172
Suicide attempts from statue,
    88
Sumner, Senator Charles, 20
Sureck, Nancy, 176–177

Tablet in statue's left hand, 9
Taylor, Major A. C., 77–78

Torch
    centennial reconstruction, 10, *11*,
        150, *167*, *170*
    lighting of, 52, 54
    major renovations of, 82, 106–
        107, 146, *147*, 150
    fund-raising role of, 30, *31*, 32,
        172–174, *175*
    See also Lighting of statue

Union Carbide, 164
U.S.A. Today, 158
U.S. Tobacco, 158

Vallery-Radot, Philipe, 141
Viollet-le-Duc, Emmanuel, 30, 36,
    40

War-bond rallies, role of statue in,
    106
War Department, 78, 79, 85, 88, 92,
    94, 96
Water damage to statue. *See* Dam-
    age, water
Weiss, Norman, 141
Wilson, President Woodrow, 82–84
Works Progress Administration, 91,
    97, 100, 101
Workshop for 1986 renovation, 9–
    10, *11*, 172, 177, *178*
World, The, 46, 48, 50, 63, 66, 80,
    84, 114, 162, 163, 172
World War I, *83*, 84
World War II, 103–104, *105*, 106,
    107

PHOTO CREDITS